Dig Shuck Shake

Fish And Seafood Recipes From The Pacific Northwest

John Neson
Illustrations By Andrew J. Brozyna

16pt

Copyright Page from the Original Book

DIG SHUCK SHAKE

FISH AND SEAFOOD RECIPES FROM THE PACIFIC NORTHWEST

Digital Edition 1.0

Text © 2016 Author

Illustrations © 2017 by Andrew J. Brozyna

Photographs are from the authors archive unless otherwise noted.

All rights reserved. No part of this book may be reproduced by any means whatsoever without written permission from the publisher, except brief portions quoted for purpose of review.

Gibbs Smith
P.O. Box 667
Layton, Utah 84041

Orders: 1.800.835.4993
www.gibbs-smith.com

ISBN: 9781423637912

TABLE OF CONTENTS

The More You Eat the More You Make	i
Introduction	iii
Growing Up Northwest	2
Salmon Hearts & Dock Rats	47
Salmon	51
Togarashi Lox	60
Hot-Splashed Scallops of Salmon	63
Salmon Cheeks in Browned Butter & Fennel	65
Salt Salmon	68
Traditional Pickled Salmon	70
Smoked Salmon Ramekins with Potato & Basted Egg	72
Slow-Slow-Slow-Cooked Side of Salmon with Smoked Sea Salt	75
Salmon Chicharrones	77
Salmon with Smoked Bacon, Wild Mushrooms & Bread Crumbs	79
Baked Salmon Belly Snacks with Deep Sugar-Soy Marinade	81
Albacore Tuna Marinated & Lightly Grilled	83
John Nelson's Fish & Chips Batter	88
John's Grown-Up Fish Cakes	91
Fish Cakes Mom's Way	93
Tea-Cured Black Cod	95
Fish Terrine	97
Best Albacore Tuna for Sandwiches & Salad	100
Tuna Gravlax with Radish & Cucumber	102
Scattered Sushi Bowl with Seared Black Cod	104
A Dog & Crab Story	109
Traditional Boiled Crab	112
Dungeness Crab Cakes	115
Crab Butter Vinaigrette	117
Crab Shell Rice	119

Pacific Popcorn Shrimp	121
Spot Roe Caviar with Miso	124
Seared Scallops with Dill & Sugar-Soaked Lemon Salsa	126
Crab Cocktail with Crab Butter & Radish	128
Sole & Rockfish	131
Poached Petrale Sole with Shrimp Filling	136
Whole Crispy Fried RockFish with Fennel & Cabbage	138
Golden Fried Sole with Shrimp Sauce	142
Poached Rockfish Fillet with Wild Mushrooms	144
Rockfish Hash	146
Bad Clam Karma	149
Mussels with Slab Bacon & Star Anise	152
Sesame-Studded & Flash-Fried Razor Clams	153
Chopped Razor Ceviche Served in the Shell	155
Sea Urchin Soup-Bowl Style	157
Oyster Bonfires & Daydreams	161
Oysters Bonfire Baked with Bacon & Charred Onion	166
Northwest Clam Fritters	168
Chilled Steamers with Lemon, Dill & Olive Oil	170
Steamers Sautéed with Sake & Nori Butter	172
Clam Chowder	174
Clam Linguine My Way	176
A Fish Story	179
Sturgeon and Dumplings	185
Oven-Braised Sturgeon with Salt Pork	188
Crawdads Boiled in Dill	190
Horseradish Trout	192
Stuffed and Fried Squid With Scallops and Shrimp	193
Salt and Pepper Smelt	195
A Story on Land	198

Mom's Swedish Meatballs	202
Fish Dumpling Soup	205
Chilled Fiddlehead Fern Salad	208
Marinated Cucumbers	210
Lingonberry & Sweet Onion Compote	212
Nori Spaetzle	214
My Favorite Tartar Sauce	217
Huckleberry Mustard	219
Horseradish AppleSauce	221
Smoked Sea Salt	223
Glogg	225
Acknowledgments	227
About the Author	229

The More You Eat the More You Make

Geno Leech

You may be a mud-sucker on a dredge down in
 Calcasieu
or bouncin' around in a Bristol Bay beer can like
 a kangaroo
Rollin' the rails under in the Shelikof
or workin' up in Red Dog on the *Justine Foss*
Fringe Benefits? Step up to the plate...
The more you eat, the more you make

You may be a set-netter up in Nushagak
or pullin' albacore tuna on a down-hill tack
If your share ain't comin' off the top
and you're more or less a workin' for three hots
 and a flop';
Take the bull by the horns, throw 'em on your
 plate;
The more you eat, the more you maket

Don't be bashful, belly up to the trough
Be it Cape Blanco or the Pribilofs
You may be a gyppo tow-boater with a tandem
 tow

Or on a Central Gulf Freighter on the
 roll-and-go
Man, stuff your cake-hole, deck-load your plate.
The more you eat, the more you make

Two splits and a life in the Willapa deep
only sleep you've had is standin' on your feet
The weather's turned sour, the skipper's
 half-baked
The frostin's done melted right offa' your cake
Can't plug the boat? Keep pluggin' your plate.
The more you eat, the more you maken

Globetrotter or troller, high seas high-risk
Spent half your life wallowin' in the ditch
Ain't got a 401(k) or retirement plan,
but you've got a knife and a fork and a bone-in
 ham
and make sure to lick both sides of your plate.
The more you eat, the more you make

Introduction

Writing short stories about my upbringing in the Pacific Northwest was a form of relaxation for a restless soul, an outlet for the saltwater beaches, rivers, and mountains that permeate my being. It is said that once you have had saltwater and salty air coursing through your lungs and veins, you require replenishment if you are away, in much the same way as the body requires certain nutrients from a satisfying meal.

My journey to becoming a student of Pacific Northwest food started, I am certain, with a clam shovel. My mother, of Swedish descent, was always willing to cook what I dug, fished, or shot, whether it became fried clams, clam fritters, clam chowder, fish fries, shrimp sandwiches, salmon patties, pickled salmon, shad roe, oysters, venison, or roast duck. The memories of those dishes are still satisfying today. My mother's restaurant career (and, in some respects, mine) began at the Port of Ilwaco, near the mouth of the Columbia River. My mother and Aunt Mildred made and sold the best clam chowder I've ever had. When I wasn't pestering her for a bowl of briny, sweet chowder, I ran the docks like a rat, in and out of the pilings, boats, and fillet tables.

This book and collection of recipes is an exploration of all that is the Pacific Northwest—its bounty, flavors, techniques, and culture, which is truly special. From produce to seafood and meats, the Northwest provides chefs with a rich and unparalleled selection of local ingredients. We even have native truffles to go with our high desert plains game and our ocean fare.

The uniqueness of my culinary offerings is shaped by the fertile land and sea that braised and flavored my childhood. My backyard was filled with opportunities to hunt, fish, trap, and scavenge and to learn about the immigrant cultures that called my playground home. As the grandson of Swedish immigrants, I learned very early about old-country techniques and flavors. Beyond the Scandinavian influences, I was also introduced to the simplicity of Asian cooking techniques as a dock rat. Since many of my relatives worked in the commercial fishing industry, I'd roam the docks and would often find myself on the log ships from the Far East, eating with the crew members and the captain. The Northwest attracted immigrants from all over the world, and over the years many of their techniques were blended into what has become an internationally diverse cuisine. True Pacific Northwest cooking reflects kitchens from Scandinavia, Germany, Asia, South America, and more. Not only have the cultures influenced Pacific Northwest cooking but the offerings of the region have also impacted each culture's individual cooking styles, creating distinctive cuisines that most people have never tasted.

I've always been a gatherer. As a child, I foraged for mushrooms and berries, dug and raked for clams, pulled oysters from the bay, and caught crab by the potful. As a chef, I've assembled recipes that reflect not only my coastal roots and Swedish heritage but the various international cultures that spice the Northwest. Bringing my food to the public included running several restaurants, from the North Coast of Oregon to the beautiful high desert mecca of Central Oregon. I went from tall fir–lined beaches to juniper-scrubbed desert. Actually, my gills were so wet from the coast it literally took me a year and half to dry out and become acclimated to the desert. And what I brought with me was seafood, and this is actually what elevated me to the pinnacle of my career. In the shadows of the Cascades, I partnered with a beautiful new resort being built, with expansive views of the mountains and high desert. After starting two restaurants and an event business, I turned my attention to promoting the Pacific Northwest through a weekly television spot, as a monthly guest on local radio, and via newspaper and magazine interviews, leading me to jot down ideas for a little book about the true experiences and flavors of the region.

Dig, Shuck, Shake presents the techniques and unexpected flavors from a native son's cooking. My food has been melded and shaped by the range of cultures and experiences I came across on land and sea while growing up in my favorite place on earth. The recipes are not meant to be cutting-edge cuisine but rather a reflection of Northwest flavors and techniques that I experienced growing up and now use in my career as a chef and culinary teacher. I once referred to a couple of my recipes as kicked-up versions of church social dishes. You may laugh, but let me tell you, any gathering organized by the wives of commercial fisherman, at the little white church next to the Chinook Harbor, was a feast!

Photo from Shutterstock

2
Growing Up Northwest

When I say, "growing up Northwest," I do not mean living in a city in the Pacific Northwest region and calling yourself a Northwesterner. Growing up Northwest is the teaching of the traditions, the ideals, the culture, the history, the heritage, and above all, the stewardship of the region and its gastronomic offerings. The absolutely unique land and sea of the Pacific Northwest are worthy of our utmost attention and nurturing. I'm not just talking about the environmental issues we all need to be so aware of and do something about. But each time you dig a razor, each time you catch a crawdad, each time you catch a salmon, and so on—this is where it begins. Proper handling of your catch shows respect to the land and sea that raised and nurtured the bounty you have just harvested.

I write about my adventures at a younger age, and the handed-down family traditions steeped in Pacific Northwest culture. I think often of what my children will become and what traditions they will carry on and how times have changed and what they may miss or not miss. The respect and care of our bounty are something I strive to teach my children. The cleaning of a razor clam or a fish, the gutting of a deer or elk, or the plucking of a bird are not tasks to be dreaded but learning experiences in gratitude and the awareness and appreciation of the circle of life.

I am unsure who wrote this, but I give thanks to the Native American elder who did:

Honor the sacred.

Honor the Earth our Mother.

Honor the Elders.

Honor all with whom we share the Earth:

Four-leggeds, two-leggeds, winged ones,

Swimmers, crawlers, plant and rock people.

Walk in balance and beauty.

How to Shake a Crab

Where I'm from, it is all about shaking a crab, using no utensils, only your hands, to extract the succulent meat. Let me teach you how so you can eat twice as much as your friends!

One of my passions is to pass on the art of cooking "Northwest" through television and cooking classes. My favorite lesson has to be showing someone how to "shake" a Dungeness crab. And my favorite comment at the end of my shaking crab class is, "You mean after all these years of struggling to get the meat out, it's this easy and I could have been eating so much more?" Let's be honest: it's no fun picking and picking at the inside of a crab leg or the body and coming out with little shreds of meat. You want chunks—whole, rich, sweet pieces of crab to dip into your butter or put on top of your Louie salad. So grab a crab, lay out the newspaper or hang out by the sink, and let's get to it!

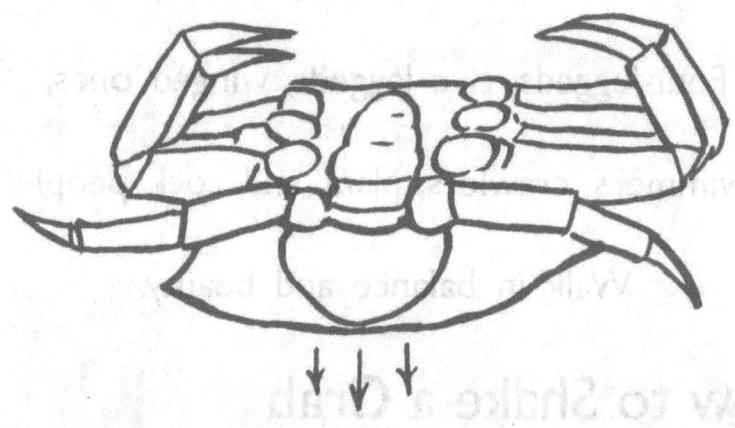

- With the abdomen up and the back of the crab toward you, pull down the very back of the shell with your thumb. We do this upside down so the all the goodies don't fall from the inside of the shell, like the butter and nectar, which can be used in another recipe if you want.
- Now that you have removed the shell, flip the crab upright and feel at the front of the

crab just behind the mouth for a hole to put your thumb in. With your thumb, pull down and remove the mouth of the crab. Right now, stop! If you find a red meaty blanket covering the interior of the body, this is the new shell growing and a real delicacy. Dip it in butter and enjoy it, or sauté with butter and garlic and a little white wine. Also, take a look for the creamy butterscotch-looking butter of the crab to save for other recipes, or just spread it on a cracker.

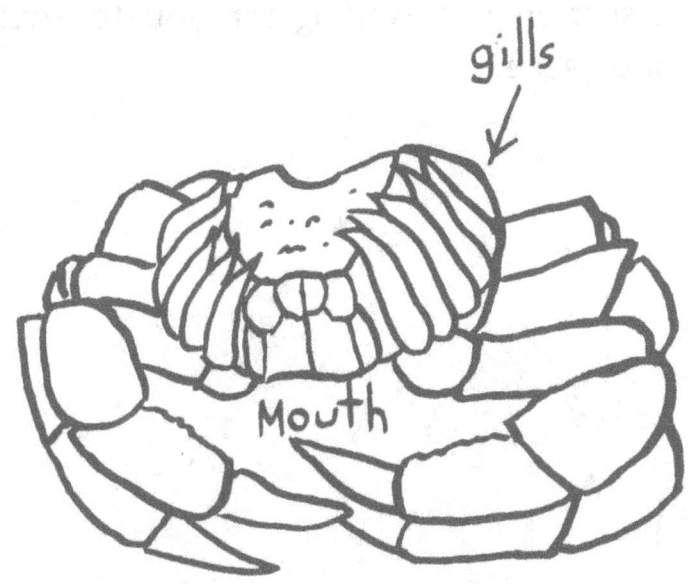

- At this point remove the gills on each side of the crab's body. Grasp both sides of the crab, holding both the legs and the body and snap the crab in half, removing the carrot-shaped abdomen from the bottom of the crab. The body meat is now exposed and ready to be washed gently with cold water. There you have it; you should have two clean halves of crab now ready to shake.

- If I were to tell you one more thing and walk away, it would be not to rip the legs from the body. Resist the urge and you will be a much happier person. If you take a look at the bottom half of the crab, you will see that each leg is sectioned with the body meat; in other words, the body is attached to the leg in a section just waiting for you to snap off in one piece.

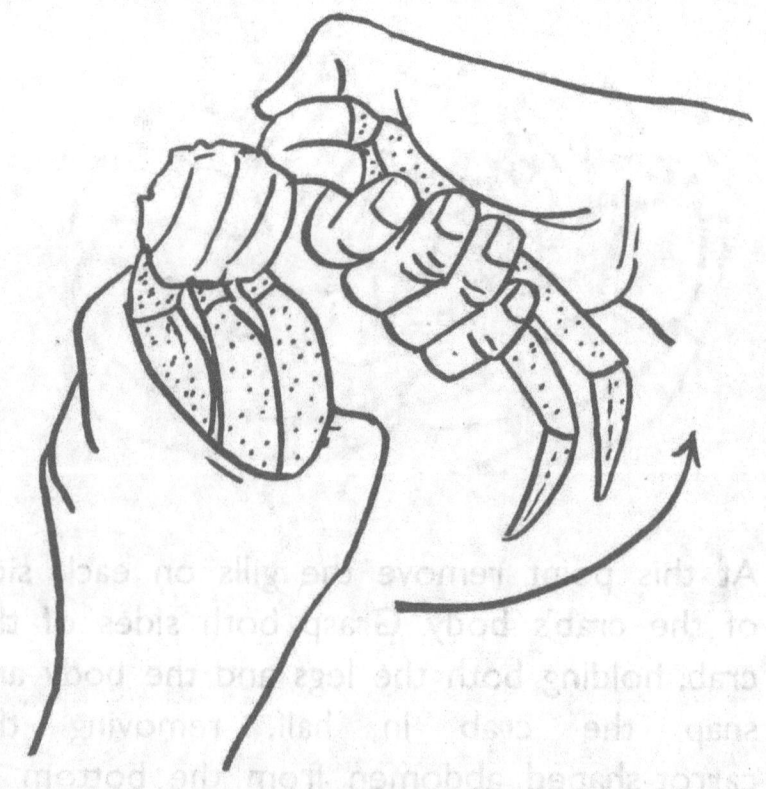

- While looking at the bottom of the crab, grab two legs with your fingers as close as you can to the body, placing your thumb on the body, and begin pulling up with the outermost hand. You will notice the body begin to separate right at the line that denotes each section of the crab. If all goes well, you should be holding on to the leg like a handle, with the body section firmly attached. Do this for each leg. Once you are finished with that, you are now ready for the "meat" of the matter.
- Grab a bowl and shake! Holding the leg with the body up, you will notice at the base of the body a pointy tooth-like piece sticking out. If it is there, grab it like a tab and peel around the body section. At this point you will see the body meat beginning to fall out! Hold on to the leg like a handle, shake the body meat out by tapping the top half of the crab leg on the edge of the bowl, and just watch the body meat fall out—awesome!

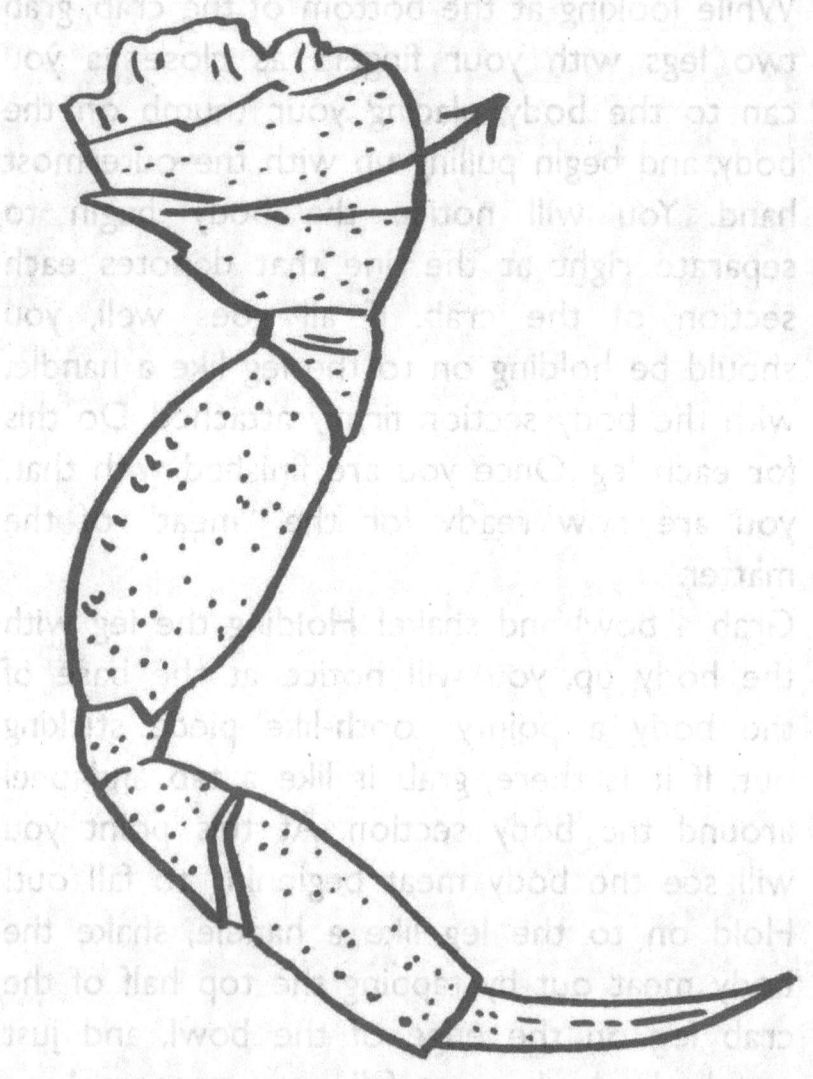

- Now that there is no meat in the body section, go ahead and rip it from the leg. Notice that the leg is also sectioned, and at the end of each section is a feather, or tendon, that runs through the center of the meat. The meat is attached to this tendon, so it is important to remove this by snapping and pulling each section apart from the rest, also removing the tendon. With the tendon removed, you can now extract the meat from the large section of the leg. The trick is to snap the top quarter of the shell with your thumb and pointer finger, left then right and snap—the top pops off. Bring your bowl over and bang the crab leg on the side of it, and whoosh—out comes the crabmeat, a whole fancy leg.

- Do the rest of the legs the same way, including the claws. Oh, and here is a little trick for the small section of the leg close to the pincer: squeeze with your thumb and pointer finger, starting from one end and working your way up as you would with a tube of toothpaste, squeezing the meat out.
- For the claws, use the same technique, and section it completely out, including the pincer. With the pincer removed from the claw, lay the claw on the table with the bottom of the U shape at the bottom. Balancing the claw right at the point of the U, give it a light whack with your fist and a score will form right in the middle. Snap the score and out comes a whole piece of claw meat. For the rest of the claw, you can use a light tap with a mallet if you like. But the important thing is to first remove the tendon on any of the

legs to remove the meat; if you find a mallet or nutcracker easier, by all means, use one.

How to Fillet a Salmon

Art can come from many different places, and one thing that never ceases to inspire awe in me is the art of filleting a fish. Standing in a marble museum hall staring at a painting that moves you is, to me, very much like watching a fishmonger, chef, or really good cook perform his or her art. I have had the privilege of watching quite possibly a hundred techniques of filleting salmon—a hundred and one counting my own. While writing this book, I started spending time with a master fishmonger with a 125-year-old fish market located in Eugene, Oregon. The fish market boasts a very large selection of seafood, which I peddle from behind the counter as I continued to expand my knowledge of filleting. The problem is, I find myself standing and staring at the fishmonger perform his art, which is very much like watching a well-choreographed ballet, while anxious customers begin to pile up to purchase fish, which gets me into trouble.

The nuances of a centuries-old technique should be really observed to feel the care and respect that goes into filleting a salmon, but I will do my best to describe it in words.

My suggestion to you as you read this and attempt to fillet is to get into character. Set the scene: You are now standing behind a large, thick wooden block with fifty years of character—an unmistakable smell of the sea, fresh fish, and just the faintest whiff of a very light bleach. You are dressed warmly with worn-out Grunden bibs and well-worn sloppy boots, standing on a cement floor that has been hosed down so many times, it has an abstract seascape pattern that reminds you of standing on the deck of the boat the fish was caught on while looking out over the sea.

With a trusted sharp knife in one hand, you grab the eight-pound coho salmon by the tail with the other hand—belly down, head pointed away from you.

- Your first cut is to remove the dorsal fin very quickly and cleanly. If this is not done with a straight and clean cut, it will show in the final fillet as a gouge. Cutting the dorsal fin off makes it much easier and cleaner to remove the fillet.

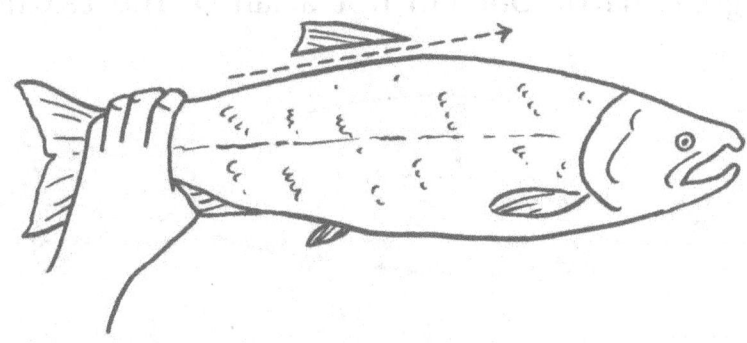

- Keeping the salmon head away from you, flip it over and, using the tail as your handle, quickly and cleanly remove the anal fin.

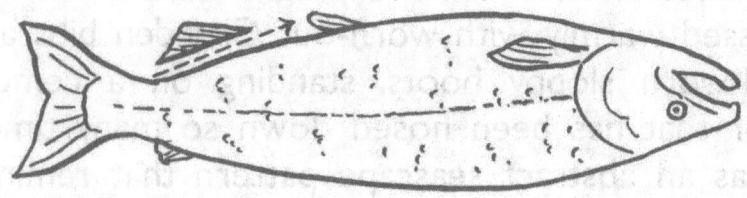

- Now for the head. Lay the salmon on its side and place your knife behind the pectoral fin parallel to the natural angle of the head. With one clean, hard push down, using both hands on the back of the blade, remove the head. Save it if you wish. (It is one of my favorite parts. Slicing it in half lengthwise and baking it with a little salt and pepper makes amazingly succulent cheeks and collar. My grandpa would also indulge in the eyeballs: great flavor, but I'm not a fan of the texture.)

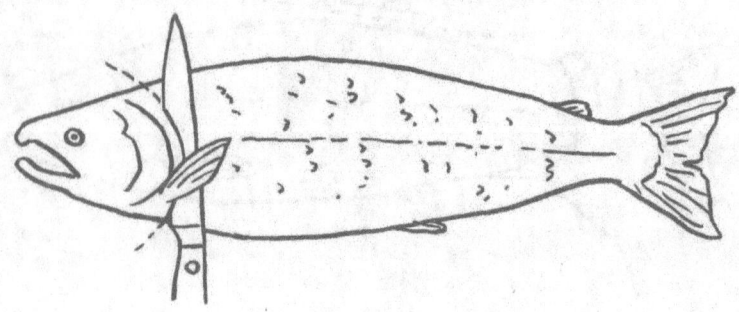

- With the belly of the salmon turned towards you, take your knife and begin the first fillet of your salmon, starting at the anal fin. Right where you cut the fin off, you will see the bone it was attached to; carefully slice the top side of this bone from the fillet you will be cutting from the backbone.

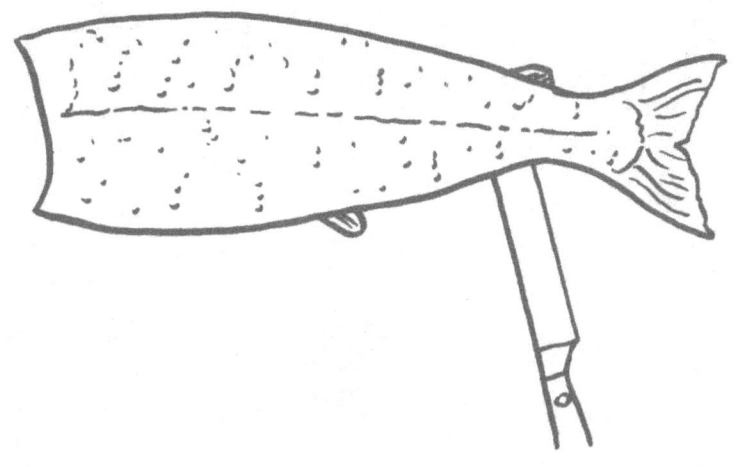

- Now, at the head end of the salmon, with the belly facing you, hold the belly flap open with one hand, and with the other hand, place the knife at the very head of the salmon, taking note of the angle of the backbone. That will be the angle of your knife as you slice towards the tail, feeling the backbone like a zipper as you slide your knife all the way to the tail. Once you reach the tail section, you will see the benefit of having cut the fillet from the anal fin bone first, making it much easier for a clean glide to the end of the fish. You now have your first fillet removed—looks good, doesn't it?

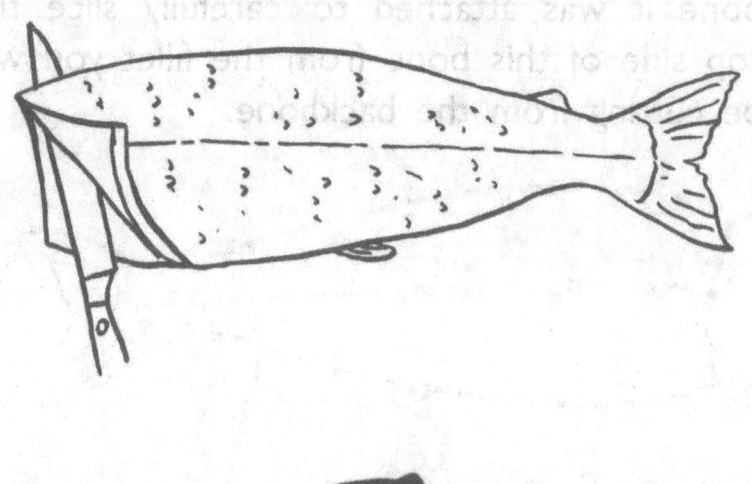

Uncle Bumpy

I fondly remember spending days on end with Uncle Bumpy at the port of Ilwaco. He was a highliner salmon troller, and his boat, the *Doreen,* having been featured in the TV series *Route 66,* was known all around the mouth of the Columbia as one the most skookum and productive trollers in the fleet.

We'd sit on the benches overlooking the harbor with other fisherman, recapping the day's fishing or just talking about current affairs. I was learning everything I could about the salmon trolling and commercial fishing way of life. Now, the great thing about this wasn't just the mechanics of the fishing but also the cooking of the fish, which Uncle Bumpy and Aunt Nanny were masters of. Most days I spent with Bumpy were concluded with taking home a salmon to be prepared by Nanny, and that was probably my first glimpse of real salmon cookery. In fact, this is where I first learned about the best part of the salmon—the cheeks. We would eat handfuls of those sweet, rich little gems, dusted in flour and fried in bacon grease. I have previously mentioned that it was very rare for our family to have just a fillet of salmon; with Nanny and Bumpy, it was all about the cheeks and salmon steaks.

- There are many different techniques for removing the backbone from the next salmon fillet. I will explain what I feel is the simplest home technique.
- 1. Once again with the belly towards you, note the angle of the backbone as you look at the head of the body. This will be the angle you will want your knife. With one hand on the top of the spine, slice from the head of the fish towards the back of the tail, once again feeling the zipper of the spine. Don't worry about removing the fillet from the backbone with one slice. Concentrate more on severing the backbone in a clean cut. Once this is done, you can go back and

very cleanly make one more cut to remove the entire fillet.

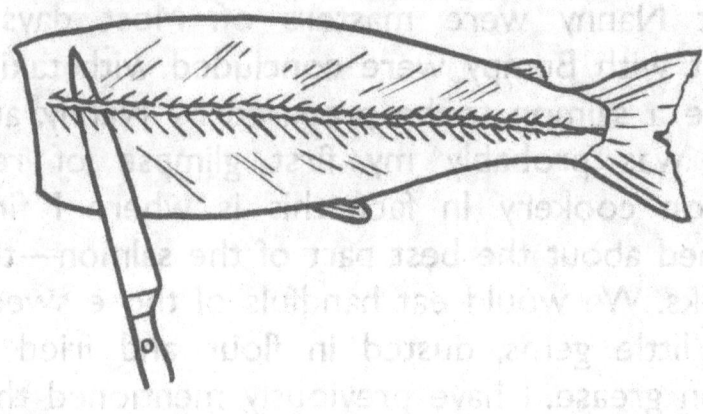

- 2. As you get better at filleting, you can experiment with removing the second fillet with the spine side on the table and making the cut starting from the tail. This technique takes a bit more practice to get a beautiful fillet but is well worth practicing.
- The next trick is to remove the belly bones from your two beautiful fillets. Start by grabbing hold of the pelvic fin and cutting it out from the belly. You will see that it is attached to the knuckle, or joint; cut around this to remove.

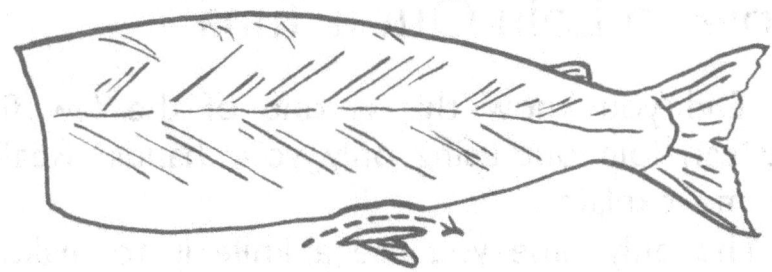

- Lay the fillet skin-side down and top, or back, towards you. Angle your knife at the same angle and in the same direction as the belly bones. Starting at the head and pushing your knife away from you (much as if you were using a wood planer), put your knife under the first five or so bones and slice them off. Repeat with the rest of the bones. This technique may be a bit different from what you have seen, but once mastered, it makes for a very clean and smooth presentation of the fillet.

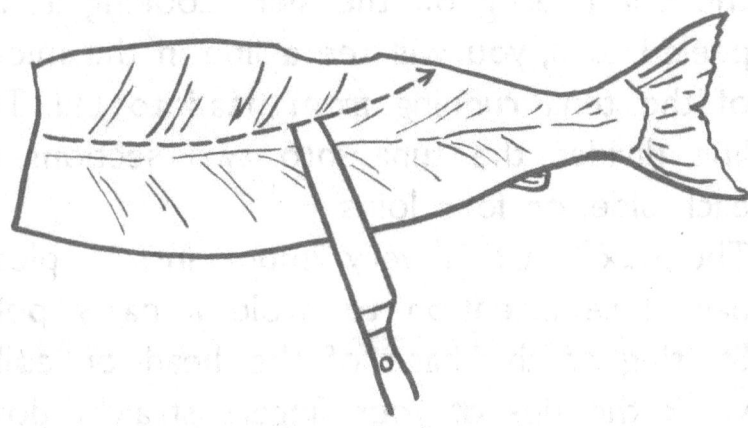

How to Loin Out a Tuna

Did you know this is one of the few fish you can loin out using only your hands? Really! Let me explain.
- The only time you use a knife is to make a cut following along the collar of the fish down the belly to the tail, making an outline of the fish just under the skin.

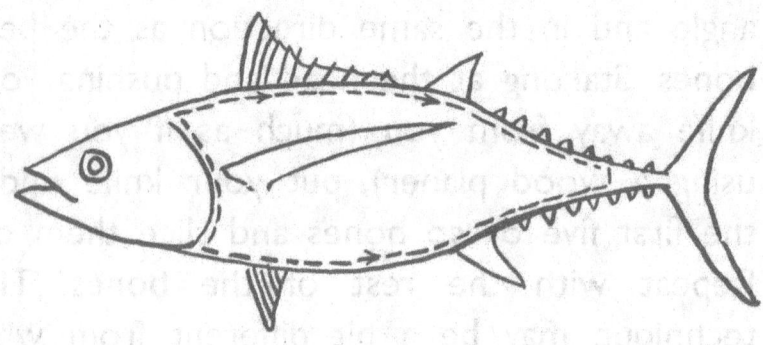

- From the collar, grab the skin with your hands and pull the skin back all the way to the tail, peeling off the skin. Looking at the peeled tuna, you will see a line in the middle of the tuna running from head to tail. This line divides the tuna into two sections on each side, or four loins.
- The next part is very important, so please pay close attention to avoid a nasty poke. Starting at the base of the head or collar, work the tips of your fingers straight down

the beginning of the dividing line until you hit the spine of the fish.

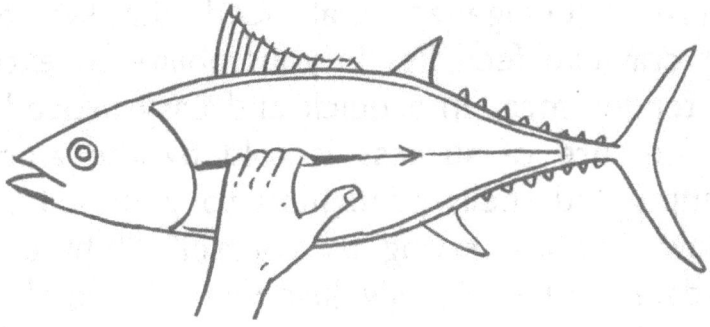

- Working your fingers along the backbone, follow the dividing line all the way to the tail. Always move your fingers back toward the tail, never forward.
- Once you have the fillets divided, go back to the collar and start working your fingers under the loin, scooping the loin out all the way to the tail. At this point you should have a perfect loin rolled off the tuna. Repeat for each loin.

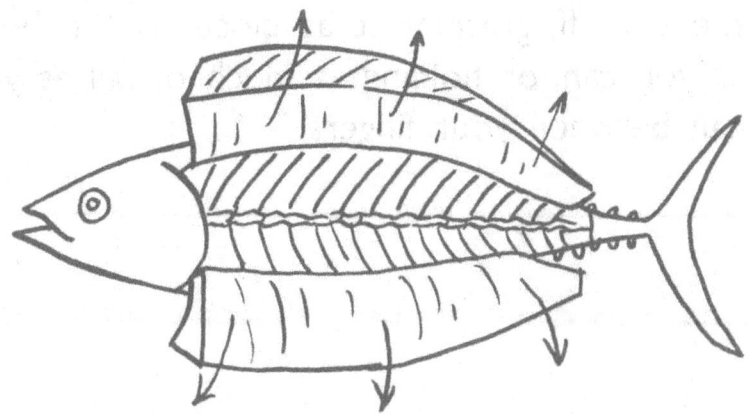

How to Eat a Crawdad

Like a Dungeness crab feed, the key to a great crawdad feed lies in your ability to extract rich, tender meat in a quick and easy procedure. The measure of success is told by the amount of empty red shells piled next to your full belly. I know you are saying to yourself, "I have had crawdads, and well, they just weren't worth the effort." Not to boast, but let's make one thing clear: this is a Northwest cookbook and our crawdads are REALLY BIG, especially those from the lower Columbia. They are much more filling than their southern counterparts and very much worth the small effort it takes to suck out the claws, tail, and body.

I begin this demonstration by saying, "Good luck and a tasty smile come to those who find a fat crawdad with roe!"

- Holding the crawdad by the body in one hand and the tail in the other hand, twist and pull the tail off, grasping it as close to the body as you can, or holding as much of tail as you can between your fingers.

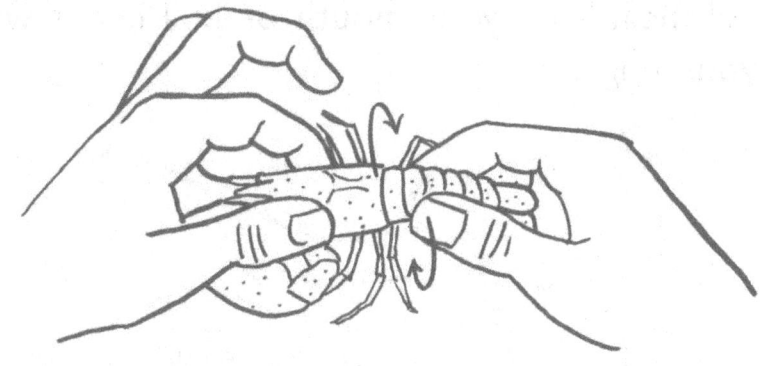

- Once you have the tail off, remove the fan, or flipper, portion of the tail by pulling it side to side.

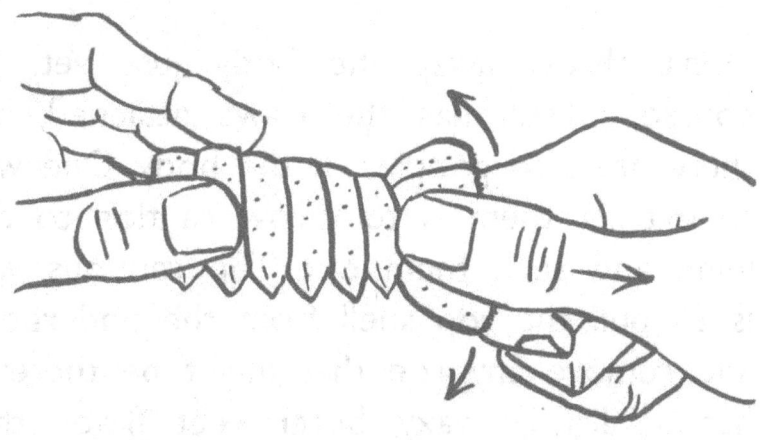

- Holding the tail with your thumb and index finger by the underside, squeeze inwards to crack the shell. With the underside of the shell still facing you, use both thumbs and index fingers to pull the shell apart, exposing the meat. Now you can easily suck out the tail meat with your mouth or pull it out with your fingers.

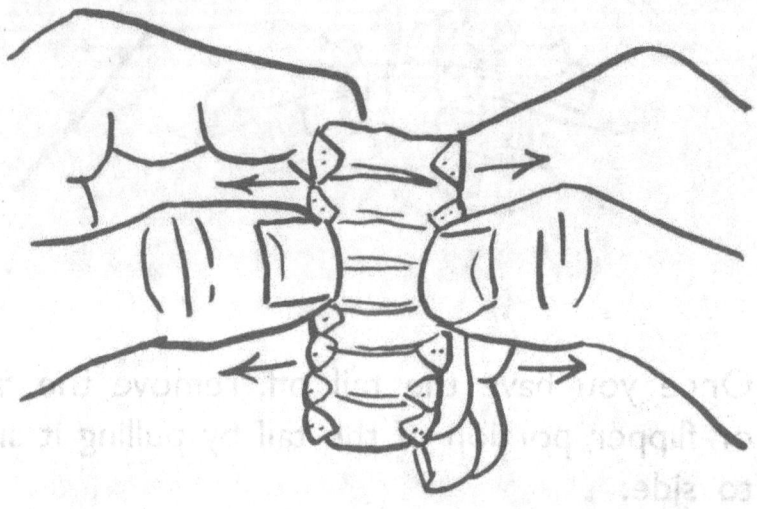

- Don't throw away the body just yet. Of course, it still has the claws attached, but there are also goodies in the body. One way to extract them is to throw caution to the wind and suck them out. The cautious way is to pull the top shell from the underbody and remove any roe that might be there; it has a slightly waxy, bittersweet flavor that will tickle your taste buds. For a real kick, go a little upscale and serve a touch of bubbly with the roe—incredible!
- Now that the body has no more value, twist off the claws and remove the lower "arms" if still attached to the claw. Remove the movable pincer of the claw; this pulls the tendon, or feather, from the meat; it is now

easier to suck out. Holding the pincer portion of the claw with the bottom of the claw towards you, bite the very bottom of the claw off, spit out the shell, and suck the meat from the opening you have just created. Repeat with the other claw, have a swig of beer, and then grab another "dad" and create your own pile of shells and a full belly.

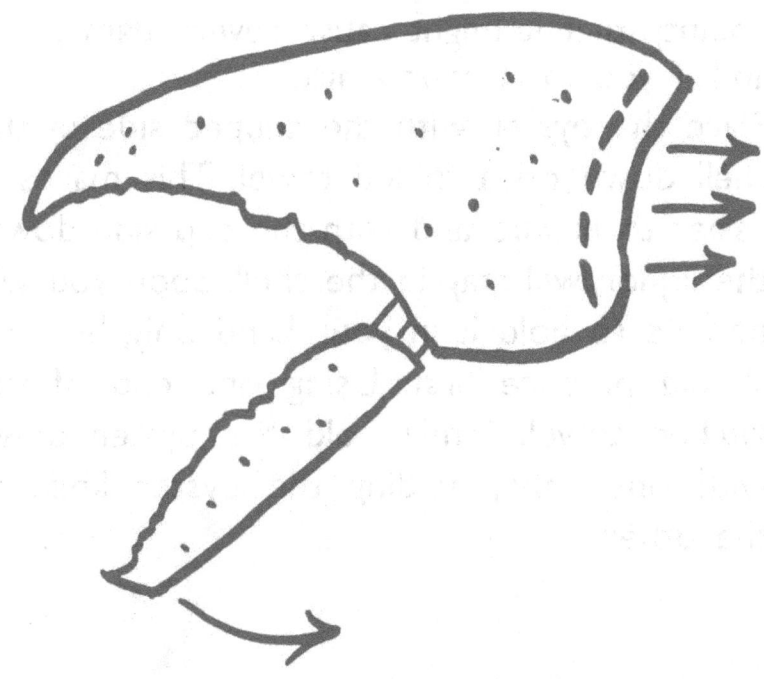

How to Shuck An Oyster

So much has been written about this subject or demonstrated at one time or another. I certainly do not claim to have anywhere near the skills of a master shucker, but I can definitely hold my own, staring at a bushel of bivalves and a bunch of hungry people.

First rule of thumb: have a good oyster knife. These are found at most kitchen stores, but they are usually too dull at the tip. The tip of an oyster knife is the business end, the part that will sever the hinge of the top and bottom shells. My suggestion is to sharpen the tip of your shiny new oyster shucker just a bit—but not so sharp and pointy that it might cause severe damage to a hand if you miss your mark.

- Place the oyster with the cupped side of the shell down on a folded towel. This makes it easier to handle, and with the cup side down, the liquor will stay in the shell. Soon you will be able to hold it in your hand only, but you should practice first. Using one end of the kitchen towel, firmly hold the oyster down with one hand, holding the oyster knife in the other.

- With the hinge of the oyster, or the pointed end of the shell, pointing towards your knife hand, find where the two shells meet. Firmly but carefully work the tip of the knife between the hinged portion of the shell. As you work the knife point in, you will feel and hear a pop. This means you have successfully accomplished the hard part.
- Now work the knife a little farther in and swing the handle towards your belly. Still holding on with the kitchen towel, work the knife in a back-and-forth motion to the other end of the shell.

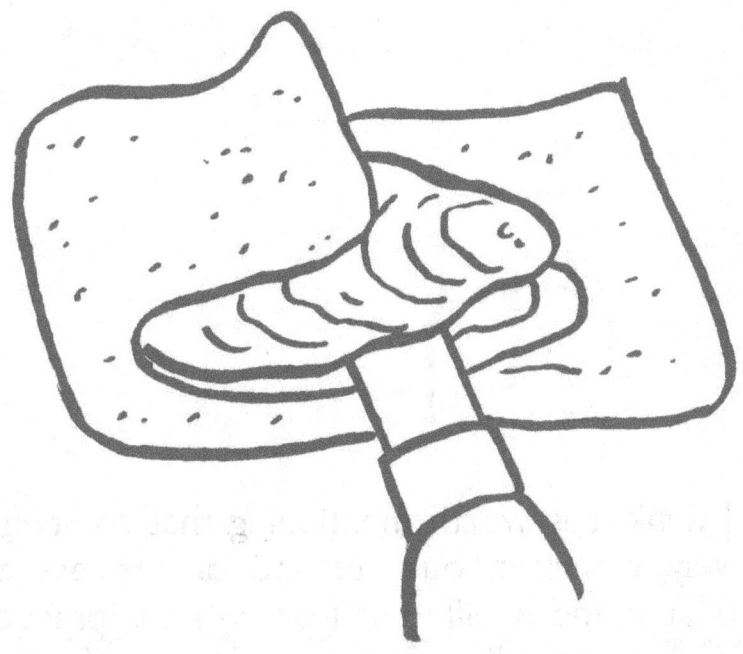

- Now that the shell is free from the oyster, pull it off. Place the oyster in your hand and, using the oyster knife, scrape along the bottom of the oyster, freeing the meat from the abductor muscle. Your flavor-packed morsel is now ready to cook or eat raw, whatever you please!

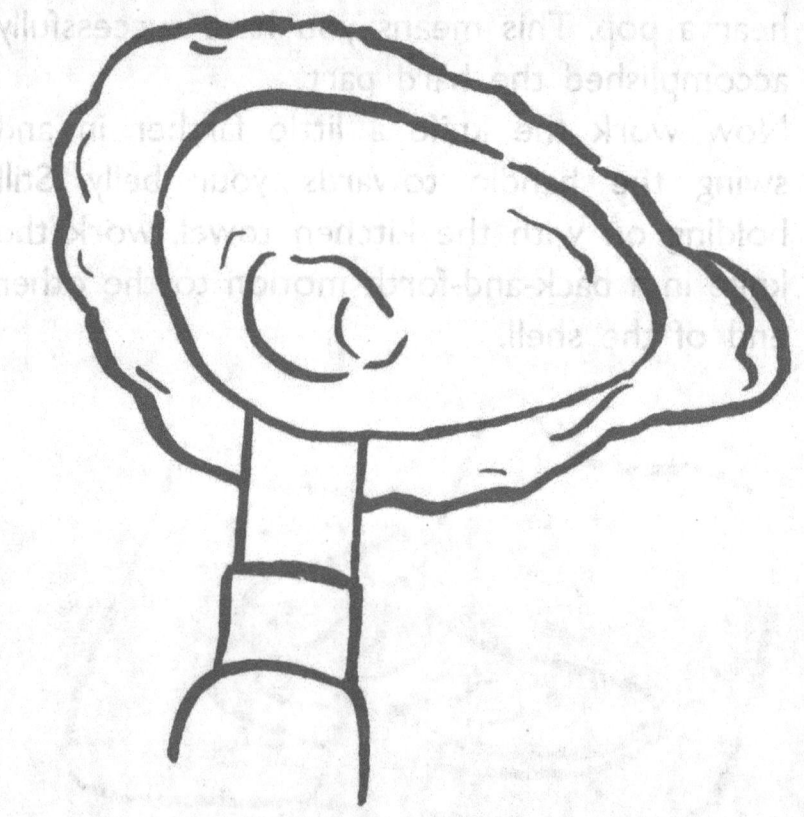

I think it is worth mentioning that sometimes the way we clean our seafood or process our meats at home is different from what is practiced on a commercial line. For example, a professional on the line will stab with the oyster knife and pop a hole in the lip, or the front, of the oyster and quickly work the knife towards the hinge, making very fast work of removing the meat. For home purposes, working the hinge open is probably the safest way to open your fresh oyster.

How to Dig and Clean a Razor Clam

There is nothing on earth like digging a razor clam! In my neck of the woods, or strip of the beach, digging a razor was veiled in beach lore like a sandbar covered at high tide. You see, if there was one thing that set a true local apart from the tourists, it was the ability to swiftly spot a razor clam hole, dig the tasty treat, put it in their bag, and move to the next hole and repeat—with the moves of an NBA forward. For myself, I have been told that I jumped from the womb holding a short-handled clam shovel and was swaddled in a clam bag. Not to mention my mom was once Miss Clam in the Seaside Oregon Fourth of July parade with me in tow!

There are two weapons of choice when digging a clam: the clam gun or a shovel. Please use whatever suits your ability. The older salt who feels the timbers creaking may find the gun is well suited. But the following how-to demonstrates using a clam shovel specifically designed for extracting the razor. We focus on three ways of finding a clam hole: dry digging, surf digging, and spotting a V.

Finding a Clam Hole

Dry digging: Spotting a clam hole is a skill that can be easily acquired or can take years of practice, depending at what level on the beach you will be digging. Let's start on the dry sandbar. On a minus low tide (refer to a local tide book), sandbars will begin to appear where the high water once was. As the tide goes out, the sandbars will become dry on top. This is where you will see the practice of stomping, or agitating, the clam to make it retract its neck and drop a hole or indentation in the sand. To stomp, pick an area of the sandbar that is clear and begin stomping as you walk. Generally, about fifteen yards of stomp walking is enough. Then you double back, continuing to stomp walk about three feet from your original path. As you double back, scan the area for any holes that may have dropped.

Surf digging: Many times, the best digging can be found in water or where the sand is still covered by the sea on the ocean side of the bar. As the sea laps at the sandbar from the ocean side, it continually wipes the top of the sand, giving you a clean slate. I mention this because to agitate the clam into showing itself, you will be using the handle side of the shovel to pound the sand as you walk. You do not want to use this method on the dry sand because the indentation that remains after tapping the butt end of the shovel in the dry sand can make it hard to see the real indentation of a clam hole.

Back to the wet sand being washed over by water. Walk slowly at first and faster as you get better. With every couple of steps, pound the sand with the butt of your shovel. Since the holes appear and disappear quickly, you need to keep a vigilant eye in about a three-foot radius around the spot where your shovel hits the sand. If you find yourself pounding and the water covers the sand, continue to pound under the water trying to create as little disturbance of the water as possible, because a clam will reveal itself by a puff of sand under the water.

Spotting a V: It is fun and easy to spot a clam in the surf. You see, generally the closer you get to the surf, the more likely the clam will be necking, or poking its neck out of the sand as the water retreats back into the ocean. For this technique, stand facing the ocean where you can get a good look at the retreating surf washing over the top of the sand. As the sea rushes back out, watch for the water to create the shape of a V, and imagine a pebble disrupting the moving water and the V pattern that it would create. Once you spot the V shape, RUN to the hole and dig quickly before the returning surf comes in—or not, and just get wet and have fun. One very serious word of caution: never turn your back completely to the sea. Always be wary and prepared for a strong wave to hit.

Using a Clam Shovel

Now that you have mastered a few techniques of spotting a hole, or a "show," let's dig! Once again I will describe how to use a shovel, because once you have mastered a shovel, it is the easiest of the two weapons.

- You just stomp back and forth a couple of times, and on your return of the last stomp, you spy a hole! Okay, don't panic! You have a shovel in hand; it is designed for "pulling," not digging. With the back of the shovel towards the ocean, place the tip of the shovel approximately four inches behind the hole.
- This next move is the most important: before you attack your clam hole, be sure your shoulder is pointed towards the sea so that you always have an eye out for the surf for your safety. Really, I've been slammed and ground into the sand a couple times. And it is not unheard of to be pulled to sea by a sneaker wave.

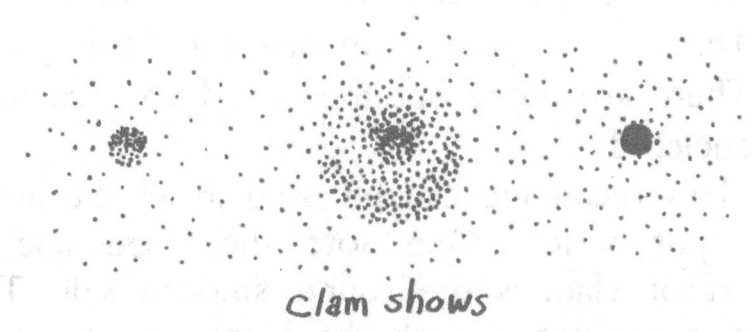

clam shows

- Now that you are safe, you are ready to plunge that shovel into the sand. Take a look at the angle of your shovel: unlike digging with a normal shovel, the clam shovel has an angled blade. With the blade of the shovel pointing straight down and the handle pointing towards the dunes, push the shovel blade straight in and all the way down to the top of the blade. Now, with one hand on the bottom of the handle (where the blade meets the handle) and the other hand half to three quarters up, pull the handle back towards the ocean, "cracking the sand" with the blade.

- Here is the cool part: Lift the shovel up a couple of inches or so, just enough to slip your bottom hand behind the blade. Once your hand is in the sand, palm side on the back of the blade; plunge your other hand in all the way down to the tip of the shovel, feel a bit forward towards the dune side, and what do you feel? The clam! You did it! Throw it in your clam bag and keep going. There are more out there, and you are now addicted.

This technique can be used in all the areas you spot a hole. One note: the hinge side of the razor clam is the round, smooth side. The clam is positioned with the hinge side towards the ocean. Digging from the ocean side lessens your chance of getting cut by the "razor" clam.

Now that you have mastered the shovel, let's take the clams home and clean them.

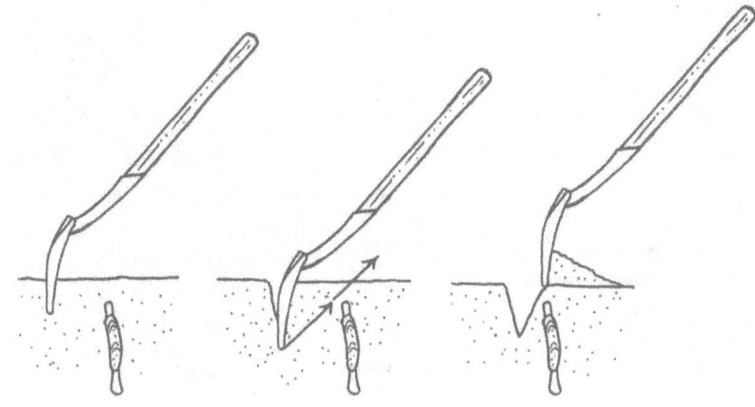

Cleaning a Razor Clam

The ultimate purist only needs a sharp knife to remove the shells. But for me, when the whole family goes digging, well, let's just say that I trained my kids well, and staring at a huge pile of clams to clean is a very daunting task. Besides, I want to get to eating them as fast as I can!
- I use a pot of boiling water and an ice bath to remove the shells. Bring a large pot of water to a full boil and plunge the clams in only one or two at a time. Once the shell has popped, immediately plunge into ice water to stop any cooking that may be going on. If the shell does not visibly pop, don't leave a clam in the boiling water for more than five to seven seconds.

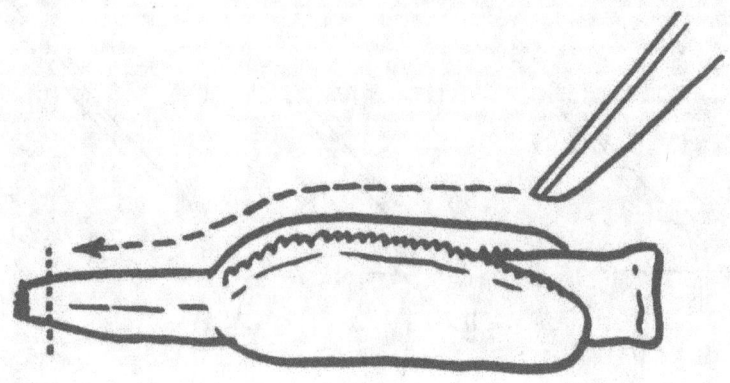

- Once the shell has been loosened from the abductor muscle by the boiling water, it's easy to pull apart and remove the naked razor clam. With a scissors or sharp knife, hold the clam in one hand, with the zipper side towards you. Start by cutting off the rosette, or black portion of the neck, just about a quarter inch below the darkest part.

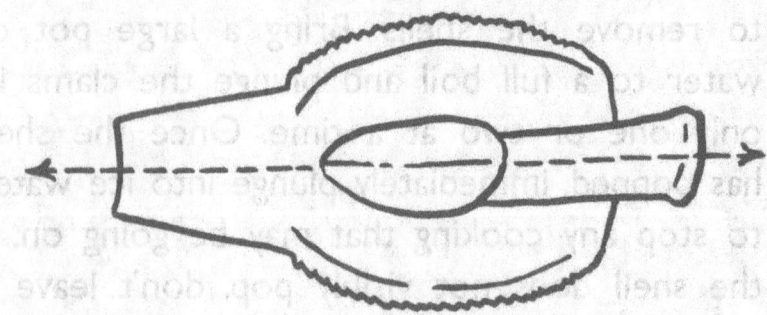

- Holding the clam with zipper side towards you, cut the clam meat open, butterflying the clam open, working from the bottom of the

zipper to the top of the neck. As you cut through the neck, you will notice two vents: cut through both of them.
- Next, cut open the digger by holding the clam neck towards you and inserting the scissors or knife into the stomach. Cut all the way to the end of the digger and butterfly it open. You have now exposed both the gills and the innards of the clam.

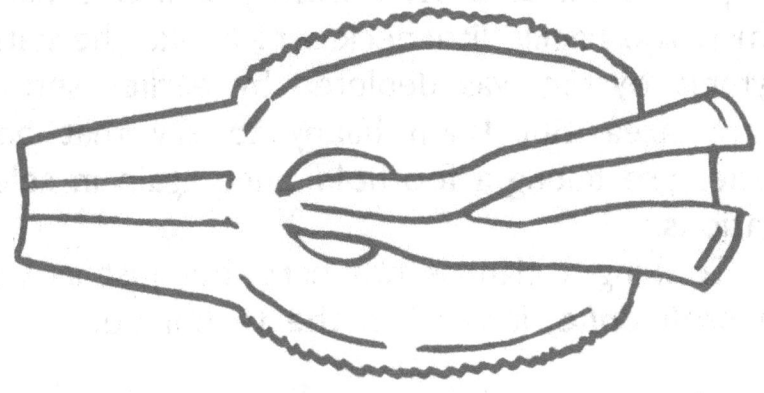

- Remove the gills by clipping with scissors or scraping with the knife, and remove the stomach pouch by pushing it out with your finger from the inside out. Rinse the clam well, removing sand or any remaining innards. One important thing: the digger is full of fat, which is not to be removed, for it is probably the best part.

Now that you are an expert at razors, go out and have fun. If you want a real experience, try night digging with someone who knows the area well. There is nothing like a warm breeze and a bright moon while digging razors by a lantern next to the wild Pacific. Kind of romantic, isn't it?

How to Prepare a Manila Clam

Before I start, I need to clear up one thing: the Manila clam is not native to the West Coast. It was introduced to British Columbia while riding along the seed of oysters from Japan. Our native clam is the Pacific littleneck, which, like the native Olympia oyster, was depleted by earlier settlers of the area. But I am happy to say that both species are taking a foothold once again in select locations.

Cooking a clam is not hard, but just as with the **crab cake,** it is all in the technique.

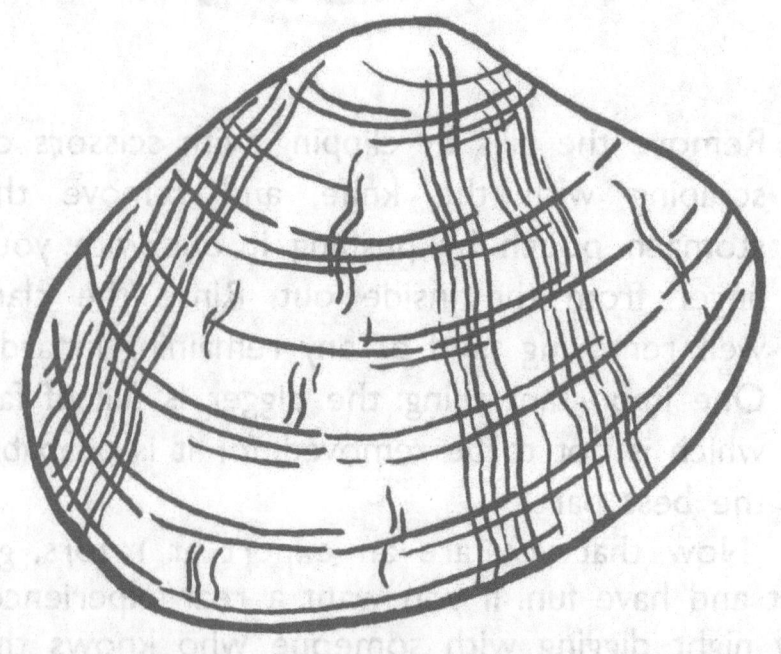

The first thing I want to stress is that the Manila is loaded with briny, salty sea goodness inside that hard shell. A large majority of recipes result in the dilution of this clam's naturally amazing flavors. The recipes I am referring to involve lots of liquid—clam juice, wine, water, stock—creating a boiling environment that dilutes the natural flavor of the clam.

- I have only one word: sauté your clams. That's right, sauté them!

Think of the Manila clam just like any other protein or vegetable that is packed with flavor, and sauté with your choice of aromatics: garlic, onion, etc. As you sauté, the Manila clam heats up, opens its shell, and releases its own juice to create the most flavorful broth or sauce you could ever imagine. Once the clams have all opened quickly, add a touch of butter and a squeeze of lemon to create a briny, salty sea-like taste sensation.

How to Prepare a Skate Wing

Skates, rays, and sharks—oh my!

Although Grandpa used to tell stories of skates so big you could see the tips of their wings on the port and starboard side of his troller, there's nothing to be afraid of here. This is one of the incredible foods from the sea that is often overlooked in the States. Unfortunate for us, because the wings, or fins, of the skate are one of the most delectable, tender, and flavorful fish portions you will ever eat! To try this delicacy you will probably need to ask your local fish market to order skate for you—and yes, they can do that. From the market, they will come already skinned and ready cook. But let's just say you were out halibut fishing and brought one aboard: don't throw it back like we all have done. At least take one home.

- First, remove the fins from the skate very easily by using a stout fillet knife. I say stout because the skate is a cartilaginous fish and you will need to cut through the cartilage that attaches the wing to the body. With the skate lying in front of you, firmly hold the wing in one hand and bend it up and down to find where the natural joint is. Cut along there and remove it from the body.

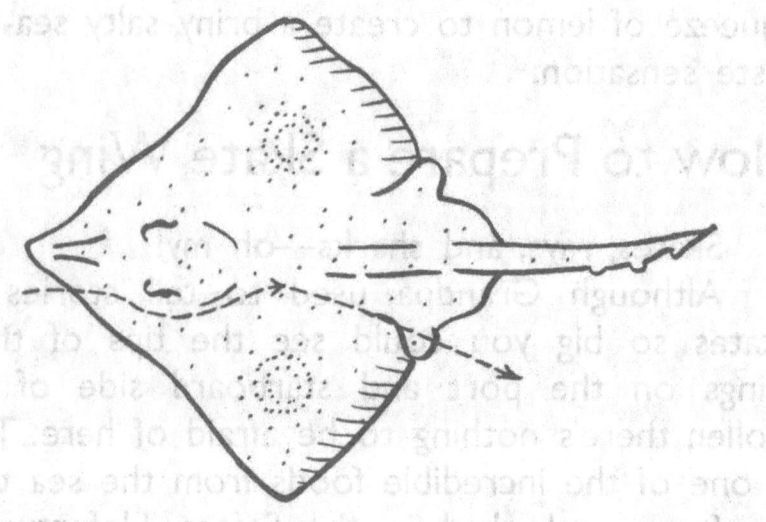

- With the detached skate wing lying on a cutting board, the thickest side away from you, remove the skin by grasping the skin of thickest corner of the thickest side with one hand and making a small cut with your knife to start freeing the skin from the flesh. Like loining a tuna, pull the skin away from the meat with your hands, working your way to the skinny end of the skate. You may need to use your knife every once in a while. Repeat on the other side.

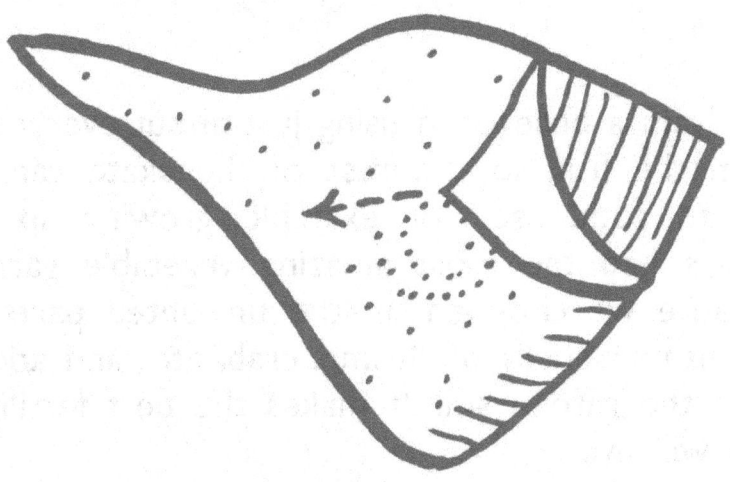

- Once the skin has been removed, you will see the thick end of the wing is a large chunk of cartilage. With your knife, remove this portion of the fin. For a tasty treat, cut this part in small chunks, dust with seasoned cracker meal, and deep-fry for a crunchy snack. From here you can either cook the wing whole or fillet the thickest portion of meat.

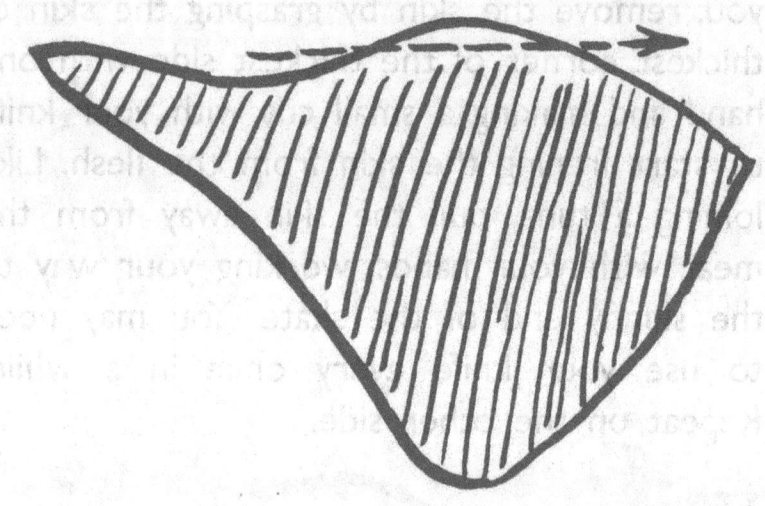

I am a believer in using just about everything from the fish, so the rest of the skate can be put to good use. For example, growing up we always had the most amazing vegetable garden because we chopped up the unwanted parts of the fish or shells of shrimp, crab, etc., and added it to the garden soil. It makes the best fertilizer you will ever use.

How to Cook an Octopus

Please don't confuse the octopus with calamari. Calamari is the name for the many varieties of squid. The octopus is in a class of its own: meaty, rich, versatile, and flavorful. I am a fan of braising, marinating, and grilling the octopus. I recommend asking your fishmonger for a two- to three-pound octopus, hood cleaned and beak removed.

I have heard of and seen many crazy methods of tenderizing—whirling the creature like a lasso and beating it against a rock, tenderizing it with a needler, breaking it down with salt and citrus, boiling it with cork. The method for a tasty and tender octopus is actually quite simple; save your time and energy. Use a flavorful braising stock to tenderize and flavor your meaty octopus.

   1 tablespoon olive oil
   4 ribs celery, diced
   1 onion, diced
   2 carrots, diced
   6 large cloves garlic, smashed
   4 bay leaves
   1 (2- to 3-pound) octopus
   Salt and pepper
   2 tablespoons pickling spice tied in a cheesecloth sachet
   1/2 bottle dry white wine
   1/2 bottle dry red wine

Using a large 4-inch-deep cast iron skillet with lid, begin sweating your aromatic vegetables in the olive oil and add bay leaves. Add the octopus, salt and pepper to taste, and pickling spice. Stir until the octopus is well coated with aromatics and is beginning to curl.

Pour in white and red wines and let come to a simmer. Cover and place in a 375°F oven for approximately 45 minutes to 1 hour. Octopus is tender when you can easily pierce the thickest part of the leg with a toothpick. (The trick is not to cook it to the point the suction cups on the tentacle fall off. If they do, you have cooked it a bit too much.) When finished, cut the tentacles from the hood. Slice the hood into thick pieces and place all immediately in a marinade of your choice. I like sweet soy, garlic, and a touch of rice wine. Immediately place in refrigerator to chill.

Lightly char over a hot grill and serve.

How to Prepare a Sea Urchin

Maybe a little bit harder to find, but still available if you ask your local fishmonger, the sea urchin is one of those taste sensations that is difficult to compare to anything else. It has an incredibly rich, creamy, heady, musky, salty, full-bodied flavor. Whether using it raw or cooked, there is really nothing like it in the sea.

- Use a kitchen towel to handle the spiky sea urchin. Place it mouth-side up on another towel.
- With kitchen shears, first trim the spikes to make it easier to handle.

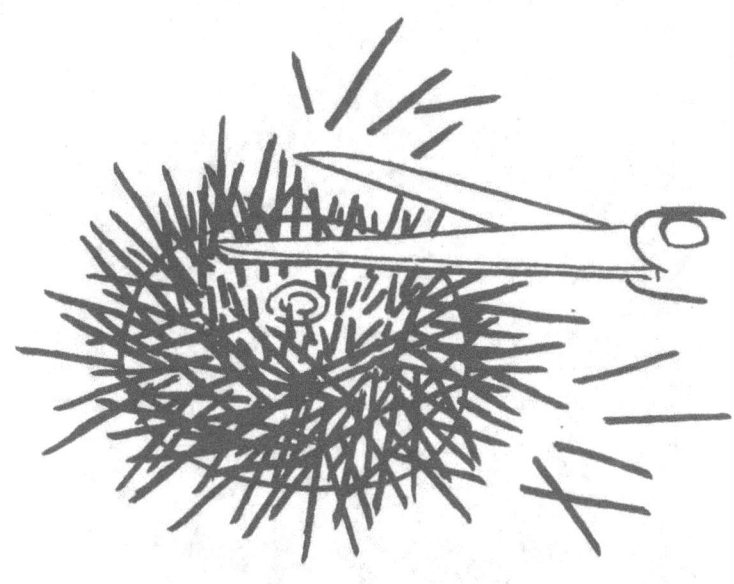

- Still using kitchen shears, cut around the top of the urchin, halfway between the middle and the very top to create a large opening. You will now see the inside of the urchin and the orange "roe."

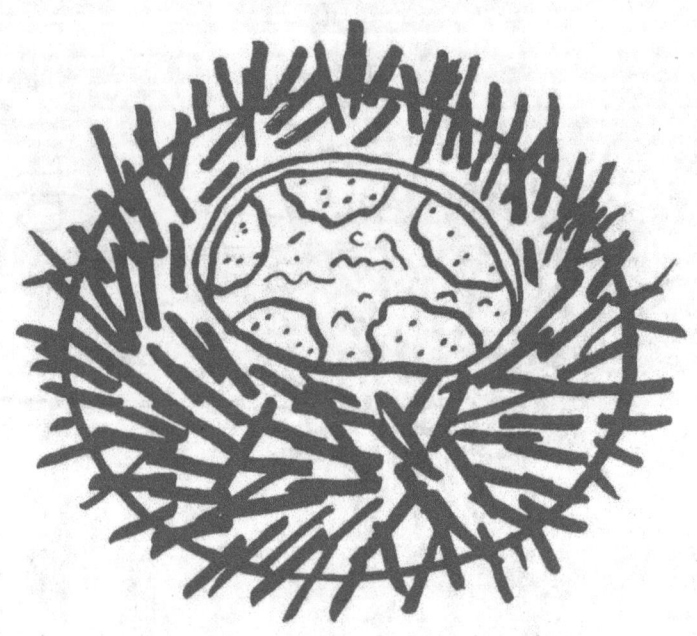

- From here, you can either poke a hole in the bottom and let the liquid surrounding the roe drain out, or if you will be using the shell for cooking and serving the roe, carefully tilt and pour the liquid out.
- Using a small spoon, carefully spoon out the orange roe and place it in a small bowl of ice water to help rinse off any of the black innards from the roe.
- Delicately remove the rest of the innards, and rinse the inside of the urchin shell to use for baking or serving.

Photo from Shutterstock

Salmon Hearts & Dock Rats

"Quick! A salmon heart just dropped on the floor! Hurry before it gets washed down the drain into the water below, and the fish get it free without a hook in it," I said. I was watching Jessie fillet salmon at a small cannery she owned on the Ilwaco, Washington, docks, where I spent a lot of my childhood. She was a salty old bird who didn't mind my cousins and me hanging around and pouncing on some of her trash.

I hastily ducked under the fillet table, dodging the other innards hitting the floor, coming up with the prize—a dark-red, slimy ball the size of a cherry tomato. The salmon hearts were ours to keep. We knew they were the best bait to catch the strange scavenger fish that lurked in the brackish waters below the cannery.

For some unknown reason, I was always the best fisherman among my fellow dock rats. It didn't matter that the fish were all inedible. I was so proud. It was 1974 and I was nine years old.

I grew up on the docks where the mighty Columbia River meets the Pacific Ocean: Lewis and Clark territory. Mom had a chowder house there, and to this day, even though I'm the one who's a professional chef, she still makes the Pacific Northwest's best bowl of clams.

I can honestly say that everything about the ocean, and everything that came out of the ocean, played a big role in my growing up. When I wasn't slurping up bowls of the sea in a spoon at my mother's chowder shack, I was hustling the incoming "pukers" for their salmon—not PC, I know, but that's what we called the guys who hired charter boats for a day of fishing. Here's how it worked: In the summer I'd tag along with my mom down to her shack. I'd get bored and start wandering the docks. I'd hang out with my cousins or visit my Uncle Bumpy on his boat.

A little cannery near my mom's shack let us kids meet the charter boats, hoping we'd drum up some salmon filleting and canning business for them. I'd wait until I saw a charter boat make the turn into the harbor. Then I'd grab my wooden wheelbarrow, which reeked of the past few days' successful haul, and run as fast as I could to beat the competition down the half-sunken dock.

I knew the cannery on the end of the dock hired devil spawn, and those kids scared me. I wanted to beat them to the money.

As we all maneuvered for the best position, I could tell which fisherman to approach first, even before the boat tied up, because I saw who had a smile on his face from wrestling with a big Chinook. That was my guy.

I could also see the faces of misery from chumming with bile for hours instead of trolling with herring.

"Hey, that is a nice fish. Wow, what a beauty! Throw it in here and let me have it taken care of for you!" was my chant.

Now I know I had an unfair advantage. I was the youngest, cutest, and probably fishiest-smelling curly mop of blond hair tugging at their hearts, pleading to let me disembowel and fillet their prized fish. Trust me, my looks gave me an advantage over the devil spawn. Think Oliver Twist: "Please sir, I want your fish."

I invariably got the most salmon in my wheelbarrow, but unfortunately, that meant it was heavier than my fourth grade–sized body could easily handle. It was my first real-life experience invoking "I think I can, I think I can" as I inched the cart up the dock ramp that now looked like Everest.

No complaints, however, because my grunting and groaning garnered great money in tips as I struggled to the top of the ramp like a wino pushing his dead '72 Chrysler to the gas station. I'm talking about 40 bucks a day in the early 1970s. Not bad for a smelly kid with a curly towhead, always on the lookout for the ultimate bait, the salmon heart.

Salmon

Salmon is a symbol of the Pacific Northwest because of its great importance to the region. Being absolutely delicious and beautiful adds to its enduring popularity.

Salmon was so essential to the survival and cultures of many Native Americans in the area that "some of their superstitions prevented certain tribe members from handling or eating the fish, lest they anger its spirit and cause it to leave their waters forever," according to *The New Food Lover's Companion*.

Chefs love salmon because people love salmon, and we can sell a lot of it! It has become the fish of choice in the United States, and since it appeals to the masses, it's more prevalent than other fish in the stores.

Of course, salmon has also become the focus of political and personal debate over the past two decades (habitat destruction, dams, imperiled wild salmon runs, farmed salmon, etc.). I'd be happy to talk about that with you over a beer sometime, but let's not spoil our appetites here. Honestly, I don't believe any other fish has sparked such ire in the human psyche as the salmon.

I must admit that I have a love-hate relationship with *Oncorhynchus* in all its varieties. We rarely ate a salmon fillet or steak when I was growing up. I learned to love the belly, the head, and the collar of the salmon. The cheeks and the part just behind the head—the collar—are incredible eating. It's like the "oyster" on the chicken (the little piece on the back by the thigh). If you were adventurous in my house, you'd eat the piece of cartilage on the snout. That's delicious. Grandpa always grabbed that first when the salmon came out of the stew pot.

Salmon is available all year because of aquaculture and farmed fish, and wild salmon is available from spring through fall, depending on the variety. You can find frozen salmon anytime.

Types of Salmon

There are five main varieties of North American salmon. Northwest Indians call them "tribes" of salmon. The three kinds of wild salmon you'll most often find in your supermarket are coho (or silver), king (or Chinook) and sockeye. You'll also see a lot of farmed Atlantic salmon.

I'm not a big farmed salmon guy. It's just not as healthy for you as wild salmon because the fish do not migrate.

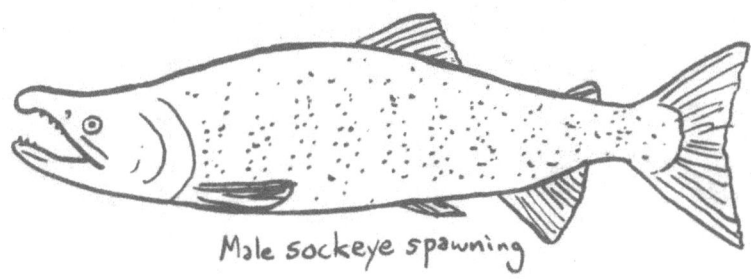
Male sockeye spawning

Salmon in the wild are anadromous. They're born in rivers, streams, or estuaries; they swim out to sea for a number of years; and then they return to their freshwater spawning grounds to breed.

Farmed fish just swim around in pens. Some are fed red dye pellets to give them more color, and antibiotics. In Chile, some of the salmon farms are destroying the fjords.

If you have a choice, definitely go with the wild because they're healthier, and know that you're also sustaining a fisherman's livelihood.

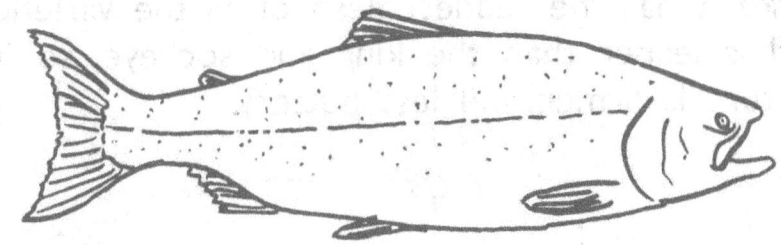

King salmon (aka Chinook): Latin name *Oncorhynchus tshawytscha*. High in fat, it grills and cooks beautifully and has big flavor.

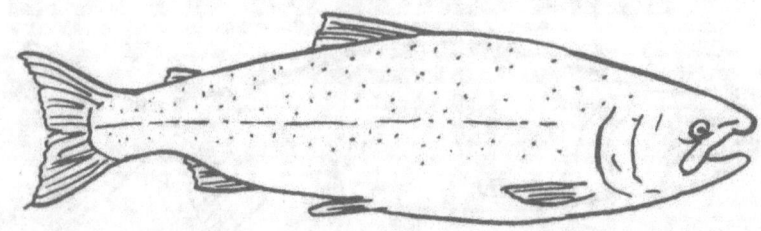

Silver salmon (aka coho): *Oncorhynchus kisutch.* Smaller than other varieties, it has a milder flavor because it's less fatty. Often striking red in color, the silver is more desirable than a sockeye because of its higher fat content.

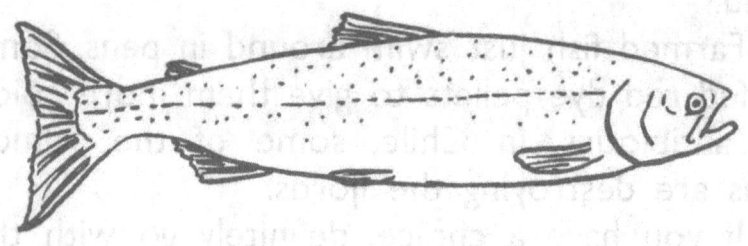

Red salmon (aka sockeye): *Oncorhynchus nerka.* It has the reddest flesh of all the varieties and is leaner than the king and sockeye, so its texture is firmer and less buttery.

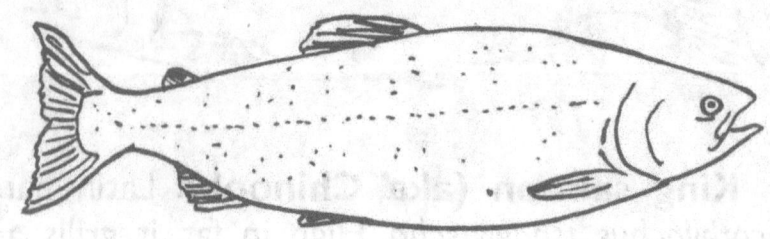

Pink salmon (aka humpie): *Oncorhynchus gorbuscha.* You won't find this at the fish market very often. It is usually canned.

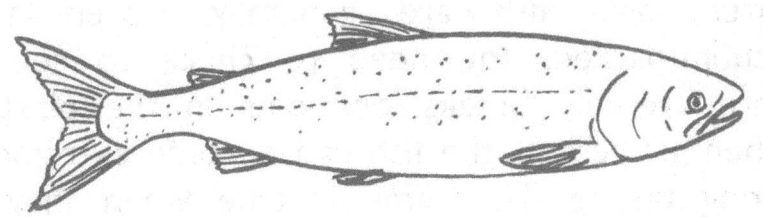

Chum (aka dogfish): *Oncorhynchus keta.* You won't find this at the fish market either, but it's an interesting fish. The name comes from the fact that it was fed to dogs by Northwest Native peoples and Alaskan Eskimos. The roe of the chum is highly prized. This variety of salmon is often smoked (and is still used for pet food). You can't go wrong buying any of the first three: king, silver, or sockeye.

Buying Tips

Fresh vs. Frozen

Fresh is best. But don't be afraid of frozen fish, or previously frozen fish. There's nothing wrong with it if it has been properly frozen. I think that eating frozen wild fish is better than eating fresh farmed salmon. A lot of times the processors will freeze the salmon "in the round" (meaning the whole fish), which is the best.

Salmon from a good troller (line-caught fish) or gill netter (rivers, bays, estuaries) will bleed the fish really well when they catch them. The fish will be flash-frozen whole or filleted and sold fresh. I wouldn't ever hesitate to buy them frozen. The fish are generally frozen and vacuum-packed. You need to check to see if there are any breaks or holes in the plastic. When air gets in, the fish can become extremely strong tasting. The same is true when they're improperly frozen.

Color

Look for uniformity in color in your fillet. You don't want to see any yellowing or browning at the edges of the fish.

The eyes do have it, and will signal freshness: clear, bright, plump is best, not sunken.

Salmon should have a healthy pink color. Wild salmon often has a deep red-orange color. See if the label says that color has been added. Farmed Atlantic salmon often has color added to make it look pinker. The colors are FDA-approved, so they probably won't hurt you. I wouldn't buy it, but it's perfectly safe to eat. Personal choice.

Smell & Touch

The best way to choose the salmon you want to buy is to have the person behind the fish counter get it out and let you smell it. Don't be shy. If you're buying pre-packaged fish, sniff it. It shouldn't smell fishy. It should smell oceany but not fishy, if you know what I mean.

I wish we could all touch the fish to feel if they're slimy (which we don't want), but we obviously can't. The next best thing is to run your finger on the plastic on top of the fish package. If it feels really soft and your finger slips really easily along the fish, it's older than you want. The texture of the fish should feel firm.

Cut

Salmon fillets are in, salmon steaks are out of fashion, and that's a shame. You know what people do when they see a bone-in rib-eye steak on a menu? They go bananas for it. It's delicious because it's cooked on the bone.

With fish, however, most people prefer a fillet. I guess they are worried about pin bones. But as with a steak, cooking a fish "on the bone" enhances the flavor so much. So if you have a chance to order, buy or cut your own salmon steaks from a whole salmon, I recommend it. You'll be amazed by the enhanced flavor. It won't taste fishy, I guarantee. It will just be delicious.

Cooking Tips

I spend most of my life around food and restaurants, and one of the things I hear a lot that I'll never figure out is this: "I'm not a big fish person. Fish is fishy. But I want to try the salmon. Could you cook that well done?"

Back in the kitchen, when we get that order, we're thinking well done will just destroy the fish. We might as well throw it in the garbage. People don't realize that the longer you cook a salmon, the more fishy tasting it becomes; and yet time and again they'll order and then eat their well-done salmon dinner. Go figure.

So, don't overcook salmon. To know when it's done, learn how to do the face-feel technique. Touch the side of your cheek, push in a little, that's a fresh piece of salmon. Now touch the tip of your nose. That's a cooked piece of salmon—still kind of squishy, not totally hard.

A thick fillet might take 2 to 3 minutes per side on a grill, starting it skin-side down. Same with a kitchen oven, but it all depends on the thickness. So try the face-feel test on your fish before and during cooking. When it feels like the tip of your nose, it's done!

As you cook salmon, you'll see a white substance oozing out of the top of the fish. Don't be alarmed. It's just cooked fat and it's good for you. You know all the talk about omega-3 fish oils and heart health? Well, there you have it.

Be One with the Fish

I've been around salmon since I was a little boy. Growing up by the ocean, going fishing, having that big Chinook on the end of the line was really exciting. I'd wonder, *Is this going to be a beautiful, bright red one or a salmon ready to spawn?*

It was like waiting for a present on Christmas morning. When I'd see that big silver fish coming up out of the water, I'd think, *Fantastic dinner tonight!*

I want it to be the same for you at the grocery store, reeling in your beautiful fresh salmon. Pick out that fish and open the package at home. Think about where it came from; it was swimming in the ocean recently. Think about what the guy went through to catch it. He probably cried out, "Fish on!" when a fish hit the hook, just like I did when I was a kid.

You should be excited about what's going to happen in the kitchen when you bring that fish home. I hope you enjoy the recipes I've crafted with Pacific Northwest ingredients and techniques to bring out the best in your salmon. "Dinner on!"

Togarashi Lox

Serves 20 as an appetizer

1 side of very fresh salmon (1-1/2 to 2 pounds), pin bones removed
Lotus or banana leaves to cover the top, bottom, and sides of the salmon
A couple splashes of vodka
1/4 cup togarashi
2 tablespoons sea or kosher salt
3 tablespoons brown sugar
2 teaspoons white pepper
Crackers (e.g., Wasa/Crispbread brand) or toast points

This recipe is a real marriage of what's truly Northwest cooking: a combination of local ingredients, an Asian flavor influence, and the Scandinavian technique of curing the fish. Paper-thin slices of this lox taste great on hardtack crackers or other Scandinavian bread or toast points.

For this recipe, you will need togarashi (also called "shichimi togarashi" and "seven spice seasoning"), which is a flavorful Japanese spice mixture made of seven different seasonings, including red chile flakes (togarashi), sansho (aka Szechuan pepper), nori flakes (seaweed), sesame seeds, orange peel, poppy seeds, and black hemp seeds. It can be found in any Asian market.

You will also need lotus leaves or banana leaves, which are also readily found at Asian grocery stores. Use a large glass or nonreactive dish big enough to hold a fillet of salmon. It's also fine to cut your fillet in half and arrange the two pieces side by side. Also necessary is a wood plank or another dish that fits inside your dish to distribute the weight of something heavy, like a brick or two cans of soup, to press down on the salmon.

Check the salmon half and remove any pin bones. Size up how much of the lotus leaves you will need to cover both sides of the salmon. In the dish you will be using to cure the salmon, place all the leaves, sprinkle liberally with vodka, and allow the leaves to absorb the vodka for about 30 minutes.

Meanwhile, mix the togarashi, salt, sugar, and pepper together thoroughly.

After 30 minutes, layer the bottom of the dish with enough leaves to hold the fillet. Sprinkle half of the spice mixture to evenly cover the leaves. Lay the salmon on top of the leaves. Evenly cover the top of the fillet with the other half of the spice mixture. Lay the remaining leaves on top of the fillet. Cover top leaves with plastic wrap. Put a plank or other dish on top and weigh it down with a brick or cans of soup to compress the fish. Refrigerate overnight. Remove fillet, slice it super thin, and enjoy on hardtack crackers.

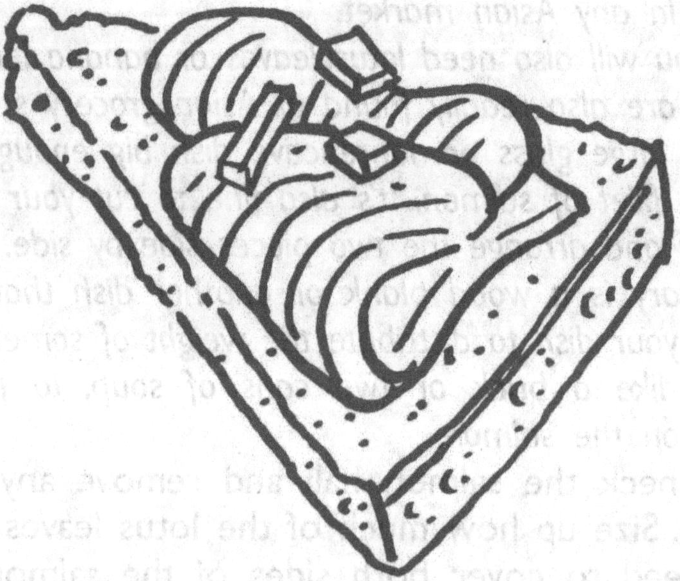

Hot-Splashed Scallops of Salmon

Serves 4 to 6 as an appetizer

1 bunch of watercress
1 bunch of fresh chives
3 cups peanut oil
Cheesecloth or a fine-mesh colander
1/2 pound fresh salmon fillet
1/2 lemon
Sprinkle of sea or kosher salt
Crackers or toast points

Another case of East meets Northwest: the watercress grows wild near the Oregon and Washington coasts. This recipe uses a technique similar to serving raw fish; however, searing the salmon with hot oil adds another dimension to the flavor—and unlike sashimi, the fish partially cooked by the hot oil has a different and appealing texture.

This recipe is very simple but requires very hot oil, so please be careful. Peanut oil has a high burning point and works best, but regular canola oil works fine too.

In a blender, combine the watercress and chives. Begin blending while slowly adding the oil, and blend until oil becomes dark green. Place cheesecloth or a fine-mesh colander over the top of a heavy-bottomed pan, and strain the oil mixture into the pan. Slowly bring oil up to a temperature of 375°F.

While the oil is heating, cut paper-thin scallops from the salmon fillet, about 1/4-inch wide; put them on a plate and sprinkle lightly with lemon juice and salt. Lightly spoon hot oil over the scallops of salmon; serve immediately.

I like to eat these sprinkled with a little salt. I roll them up and pop them in my mouth, but they're also good on crackers or toast points.

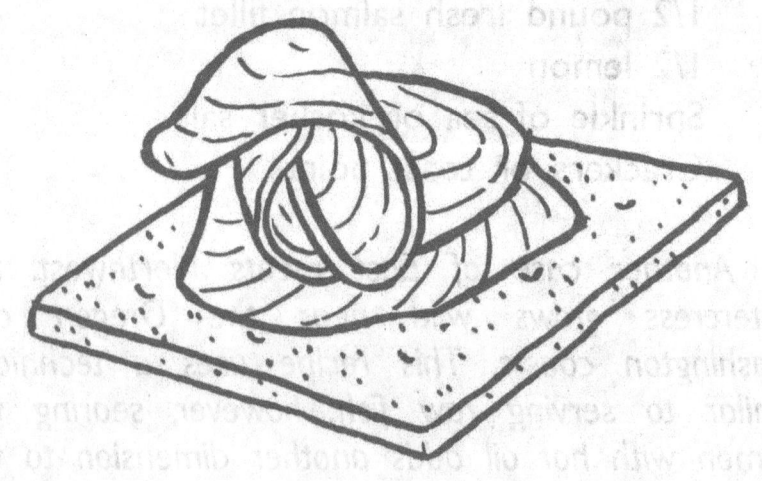

Salmon Cheeks in Browned Butter & Fennel

Serves 4 as an appetizer

2 tablespoons unsalted butter, divided
2 teaspoons pickling spice
1/2 pound salmon cheeks
Unbleached all-purpose flour, for dredging
1/2 bulb fennel, thinly sliced
Sea or kosher salt
Freshly ground black pepper
3 tablespoons anisette liqueur (Ouzo or Pernod)
1/4 lemon, squeezed

When I was growing up, it was a fairly rare occasion for a fillet of salmon to be on our dinner table. Fillets were used for canning, pickling, and smoking. Instead, on the pedestal of holy fishdom at my house were the cheeks, bellies, and collars of the salmon. We baked these, and we made stews out of the fish heads. If we ever cooked a whole salmon, we'd eat the belly, collar, and tail first, leaving a lot of the fillet. Mom would make salmon cakes with the leftovers the next morning, and we'd have them with eggs and potatoes. Good stuff.

Ask your seafood counter manager to order some salmon cheeks for you. They can get them—trust me.

Add 1 tablespoon of butter and the pickling spice to a large sauté pan on medium-high heat. Once the butter has browned, strain the pickling spice out and return the butter to the pan.

Dredge the salmon cheeks in the flour, and when the pan is back up to moderate heat, add the cheeks to the brown butter, along with the sliced fennel, and salt and pepper to taste. Sauté until the checks are slightly brown and the fennel is tender-crisp. Add the anisette and lemon juice to the pan and allow to reduce slightly for about 3 minutes. Add the remaining tablespoon of butter to the pan and incorporate well with the sauce. It's ready to serve.

A great side dish is **Nori Spaetzle,** a Swiss/Bavarian/German noodle, or dumpling, with an Asian twist from the addition of seaweed (nori).

Salt Salmon

Rock salt
Salmon fillet, skin on, cut to fit your container

One of the best things about going to visit Grandpa John (for I was named) on the Long Beach peninsula of the Washington coast was his tool shed. Sure, the tools were great, but lining the shelves next to them were many clear glass jars of salt salmon. Those jars were just as exciting to me as the tools, because I knew they would soon be turned into pickled salmon and other tasty treats.

Line the bottom of a nonreactive container (preferably glass) with about 1/2 inch of salt.

Place large cut pieces of salmon into the container skin-side down, enough to cover the salt. Top the first layer of salmon with another 1/2 inch of salt. Repeat the steps, making sure when you layer the salmon that the layers are skin-to-skin and meat-to-meat. As the salt melts, some of the salmon pieces may touch each other, and if this happens, you want to keep any fish scales away from the meat, making for a more appetizing final product.

Allow the salmon to cure in salt in the refrigerator for at least a week, although I think some of Grandpa's were on the shelf for a year or more! Remember, I'm alive and well to share this recipe, so have no fear! Use the salt salmon to make **Traditional Pickled Salmon.**

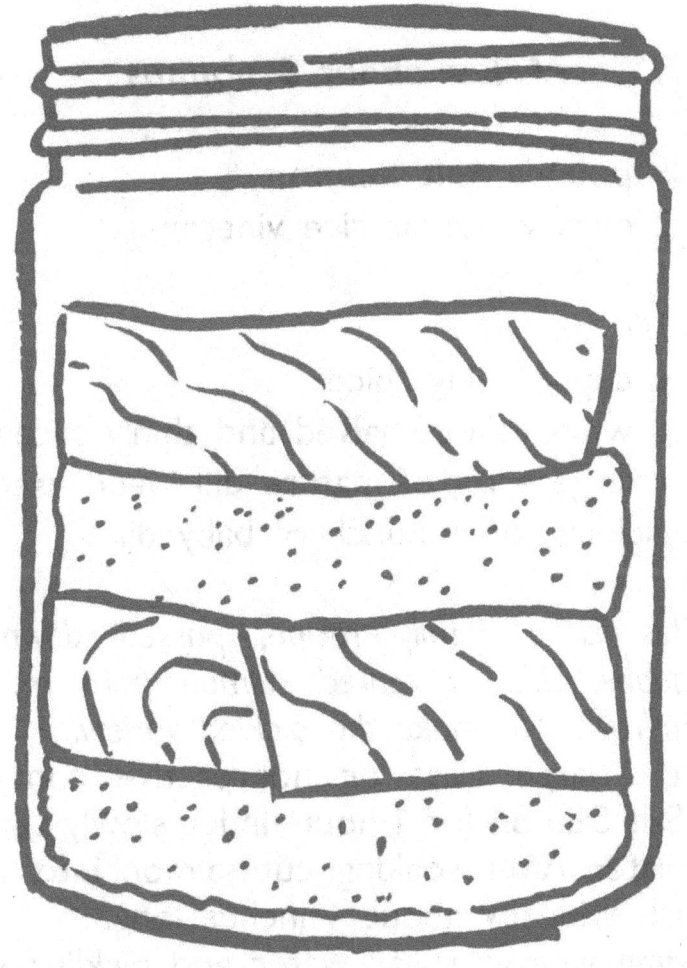

Traditional Pickled Salmon

Makes about 5 pounds

5 pounds **Salt Salmon**
2 cups white or rice vinegar
1 cup sugar
1/2 cup water
1 cup pickling spice
1 white onion, halved and thinly sliced
1 large sprig of mature dill weed used for pickling, or 1 bunch of baby dill

This is a family recipe, passed down for generations. Use the cured salmon from my Salt Salmon recipe to make the pickled variety.

In a large glass or nonreactive container, soak Salt Salmon for 1 hour under slowly running cold water. After soaking, cut salmon into strips 1/2 inch wide by about 4 inches long.

Bring vinegar, sugar, water, and pickling spice to a boil; then let it cool in the refrigerator.

While the pickling mixture is cooling, randomly pack salmon, onion, and dill into a nonreactive container. Pour the cooled pickling spice mixture over the salmon, onion, and dill. Cover and place in the refrigerator for about 5 days. The longer it's there, the more flavor the salmon will absorb.

Use clean utensils to fish out salmon pieces and onion from the container. Your fingers have bacteria on them that will shorten the life of your delicious pickled salmon. I like to chow down on pickled salmon by itself, but it's good on hardtack crackers or the round wheels of Scandinavian bread found in specialty food stores.

Smoked Salmon Ramekins with Potato & Basted Egg

Serves 4

Butter, for sautéing and for rubbing inside ceramic dishes
4 tablespoons minced onion
2 cups leftover baked or boiled potatoes, peeled and grated
Kosher or sea salt
Freshly ground black pepper
1 tablespoon finely chopped baby dill
8 ounces good-quality smoked salmon
4 teaspoons heavy cream
4 eggs

This makes a great breakfast-in-bed surprise for Mom or Dad on a birthday or Mother's or Father's Day, or a perfect brunch item for the holidays. I developed this recipe remembering my mom's delicious salmon hash. Something else mom was good at was seafood biscuits and gravy: shrimp or crab or fish and a hard-boiled egg chopped up in the gravy. Now that's a good Pacific Northwest breakfast.

You will need 4 ovenproof ceramic baking dishes up to 1-1/2 inches deep and 3-1/2 inches across.

Preheat oven to 350°F.

Melt a tablespoon of butter in a large pan over moderate heat and sauté the minced onion until slightly browned. Add the potatoes and continue to sauté, stirring until the onions are mixed in well. Add salt and pepper to taste and dill and remove from the heat.

Butter the insides of the ceramic dishes. Divide the potato mixture evenly among the four dishes. Top the potatoes with equal portions of smoked salmon. Pour a teaspoon of cream over each dish. Carefully crack 1 egg on top of each dish. Place the dishes on a baking sheet in the oven and bake until desired doneness of the egg (about 5 to 7 minutes for a runny egg, or about 8 to 10 minutes for a firmer yolk).

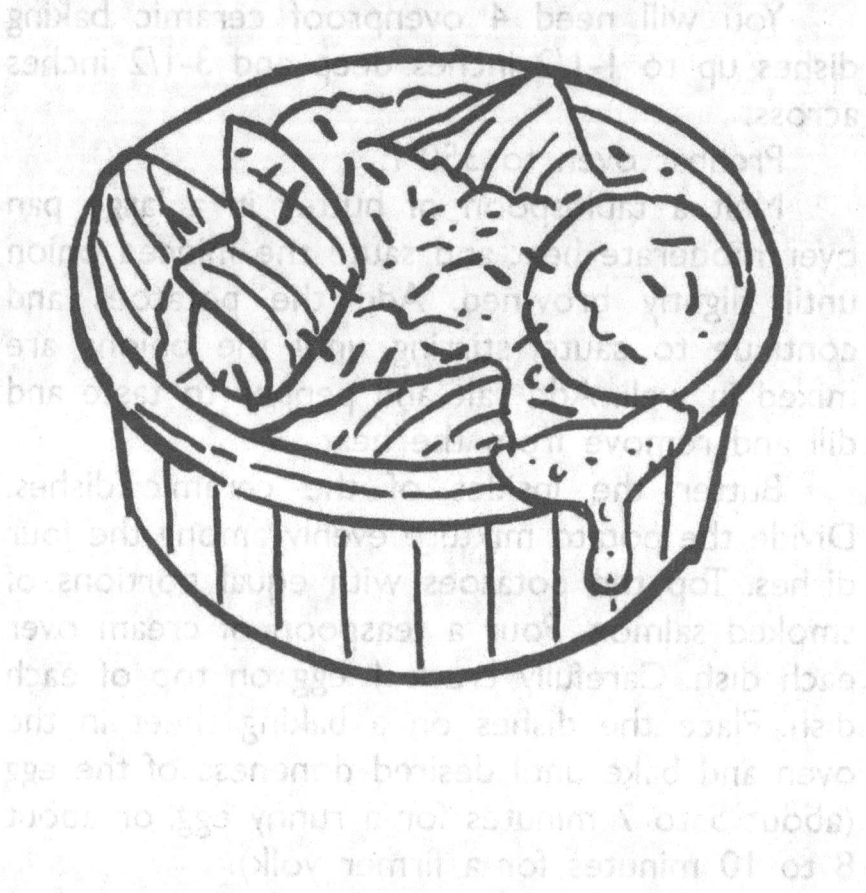

Slow-Slow-Slow-Cooked Side of Salmon with Smoked Sea Salt

Serves 4 to 6

1 (2 to 3 pound) fresh salmon fillet, skin on
1 cup extra virgin olive oil
2 tablespoons **smoked sea salt**

This cooking method creates a very buttery texture and rich taste that you must try with your next fresh fillet of salmon. The slow cooking technique is reminiscent of the Native American salmon bake, where the fish fillet is cooked on a wooden frame before an open fire for an hour or more. The slow, slow cooking at a low temperature warms the fish all the way through and results in that unbelievably buttery texture.

Cut the salmon just so it will fit in your baking dish, or you can use foil and a sheet pan for the whole fillet.

Cover the bottom of your baking dish with 1/2 cup of the olive oil.

Lay the salmon skin-side down on top of the oil. Pour the rest of the oil on top of the salmon. Allow the salmon to rest and absorb some of the oil for about 1 hour in the refrigerator.

Preheat the oven to 185°F. No convection ovens for this recipe.

Bake the salmon for about 45 minutes, or until the fillet yields to a slight press of the finger.

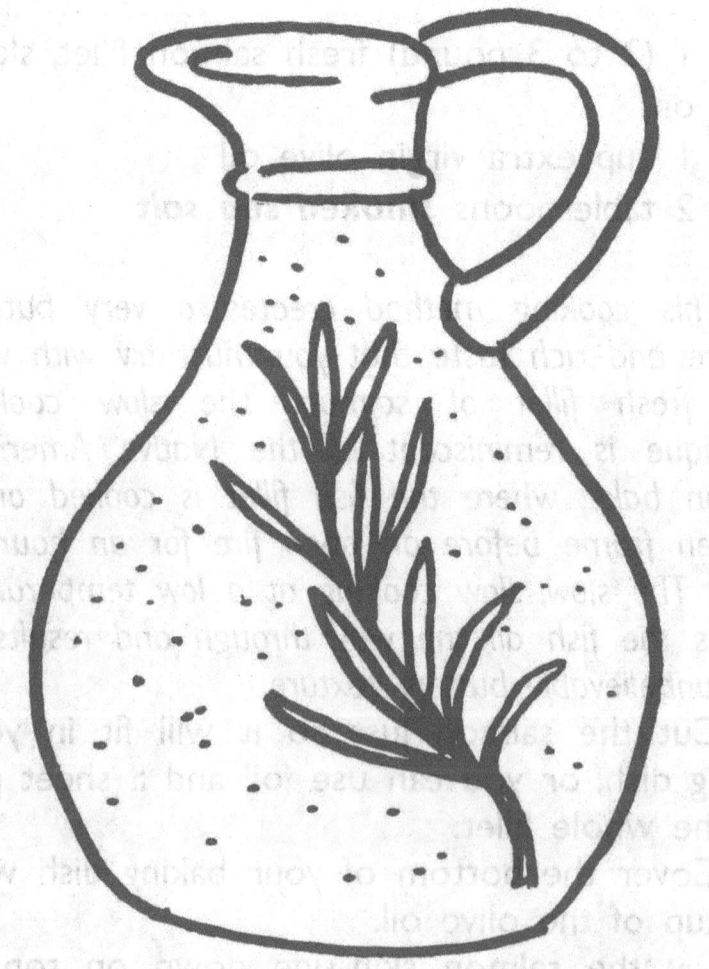

Salmon Chicharrones

Serves 4

Skin from 1 side of raw salmon
3 tablespoons kosher or sea salt
1 tablespoon freshly ground black pepper
About 3 cups peanut or canola oil

A *chicharron is a deep-fried pork rind treat that you can find in Latin American markets. Deep-frying makes a lot of things taste great. So don't ever throw away raw salmon skin; make salmon chicharrones! I like putting some on my salad with* **Crab Butter Vinaigrette** *—decadent! They're salty, crispy, and a little fishy, but it's a rich fish flavor that's surprisingly neither fatty nor greasy.*

My main guy in the kitchen at Brasada Ranch is from Seaside, Oregon—my neck of the woods. When I interviewed him, I told him I'd give him a try for a week. The first day, he took some salmon skin and made deep-fried "salmon rinds." I couldn't believe it. I said, "How'd you know that's the best part of the salmon? Nobody does that around here but me." I thought, This is the guy for me. That was his job interview, basically. Make salmon chicharrones for me, and you're hired!

Lay out the salmon skin scale-side down, and with a knife, remove any extra fat or meat.

Sprinkle salt and pepper evenly on both sides of the skin and let it stand on a rack for 10 to 15 minutes. In a large, heavy pot, add about 1 inch of oil and heat to 325°F.

While the oil is heating, brush off any extra salt and pepper, and cut the salmon skin crosswise into 1 1/2-inch-wide strips. Gently place about 12 strips of skin in the hot oil and deep-fry them until all bubbles stop coming from the skin. Remove skin from the oil and place it on paper towels to drain. Once cooled, the skin will be crispy and delicious. Eat it like popcorn or pork rinds, or scatter it on a salad.

Salmon with Smoked Bacon, Wild Mushrooms & Bread Crumbs

Serves 4

1 side of fresh salmon (1-1/2 to 2 pounds), skin on
3 cups day-old hearty bread (whole grain, French or sourdough)
1 pound wild mushrooms, like chanterelles
1/4 cup chopped fresh chives
2 tablespoons chopped fresh dill
3 anchovy fillets
Kosher or sea salt
Freshly ground black pepper
1/2 cup olive oil
1/2 pound smoked crisp bacon

This combination of flavors is like taking in all the tastes and smells of the Northwest at once, from salmon on the docks, to fresh bread baking in a wood burning stove on a rainy day, to the smell of the damp forest that the mushrooms call home.

I developed this recipe after travels to Mexico. I went out fishing with the small commercial fishermen in their panga boats and often came back with little halibut. The hotel owner would bake them for me for dinner. She'd grind up bacon, chiles, and breadcrumbs, add capers and garlic, then slather it all over the fish and bake it. Delicious! That was my inspiration for this recipe using Northwest mushrooms.

Preheat the oven to 350°F. Grease a sheet pan with olive oil or spray it with cooking spray.

Place the salmon skin-side down on the sheet pan.

Put the bread, mushrooms, chives, dill, anchovies, and salt and pepper to taste into a food processor; blend until chunky. Add the olive oil and bacon and blend a little more, until the bacon turns to small crumbles and the olive oil has bound everything together.

Spread this mixture on top of the salmon and bake it for about 12 to 15 minutes, or until the fillet feels just firm to the touch.

Baked Salmon Belly Snacks with Deep Sugar-Soy Marinade

Serves 4 as an appetizer

1 cup palm sugar or brown sugar
2 cups dark soy sauce (mushroom soy is great, available at Asian grocery stores)
1/4 cup white vinegar
1 tablespoon coarse black pepper
Salmon belly from 1 whole salmon fillet (about 1/2 pound), skin on

Besides the cheeks, the belly is the richest and most flavorful part of the salmon. This is a great late-night snack to enjoy while watching surfing videos.

If you are unsure of how to trim the salmon belly from fillet, ask your fishmonger to do it.

In a ziplock bag, add all the ingredients except the salmon and mix well.

Cut the salmon belly into 2-inch pieces with the skin on, and add to the marinade bag. Put the bag in the refrigerator overnight.

Preheat oven to 250°F.

Place the salmon belly pieces on a rack positioned on top of a sheet pan to catch the drips. Bake the salmon for at least 1 hour and up to 90 minutes, or until the meat is very firm and all the "give" is gone when you push the meat with your finger.

The belly snacks can be eaten warm, but I think they taste best after they have cooled completely in the refrigerator.

Albacore Tuna Marinated & Lightly Grilled

Serves 4 to 6

1 teaspoon of sambal (a chili-based sauce found in the Asian food section)
1/4 cup orange juice
1 teaspoon caraway seeds
1-1/2 teaspoons coarse salt
1/4 cup olive oil
1 fresh loin of tuna (about 1 to 1-1/2 pounds)

Tuna, one of the fastest fish in the sea, is also one of the fastest to cook. So watch it carefully on the grill and don't overdo it on the heat.

Mix all of the ingredients together, from the sambal to the olive oil, and marinate the tuna loin in it for no more than 1 hour, or the citrus will begin to "cook" the fish and you will have ceviche.

Start your grill by wiping the grates down with a bit of olive oil, and let it come to a high temperature.

Grill each side of the tuna for about 1 minute, or just long enough to caramelize the sugars in the marinade. The middle of the tuna should still be medium to medium-rare for the best flavor. After you take it off the grill, let the tuna rest on a plate for a few minutes before serving.

Buying Tip for Albacore Tuna

In albacore tuna, the chicken of the sea, it is actually quite easy to distinguish between a fresh and not-so-fresh fish. When inspecting a whole fish, as with most fish, the eyes have it. The eye of the albacore tuna is particularly large, making it very easy to tell whether it is fresh is not. The eyes should be clear and a bit plump, not sunken. Also, the smell should be of the sea, not of the fish, and the skin should be slick but not slimy or dry.

When buying fresh loins of albacore, the color is what to look for. A fresh loin has a white and very slight pink hue to it. Not to be confused with its southern Pacific counterpart, the tombo tuna, a larger albacore that has a different diet, and is very pink to almost red in color. As the albacore ages, it will take on a brown tint and gray up just a bit. Although a hint of brown doesn't mean it is bad, it is getting on in age and should be consumed immediately.

Fish and Chips Northwest Style

A great fish and chips is the same as a great bowl of clam chowder for me—a taste sensation that dances on my tongue, reminding me of the salty sea air and childhood events that shaped my spiritual essence. Okay, you may be thinking at this point that I might have a bit too much sand behind (or between) my ears, but fish and chips is an art, and when made it's made with fresh Northwest fish, it's "skookum" ("awesome," in Chinook slang)!

It's like most anything; if you have not seen, felt, or tasted something in its true and proper form, you won't know what you've been missing. Case in point, I can't begin to tell you how many of my restaurant guests tell me they think that fish is "fishy," or oysters are "gross," and how many have allowed me to indulge their senses by preparing the food they think they don't like properly, and giving them a taste. I love to watch as "aha!" moments light up their faces and they are converted to seafood lovers. It's the same with fish and chips. Once you know what a delight this classic can truly be, an "aha!" moment might just creep up on you too.

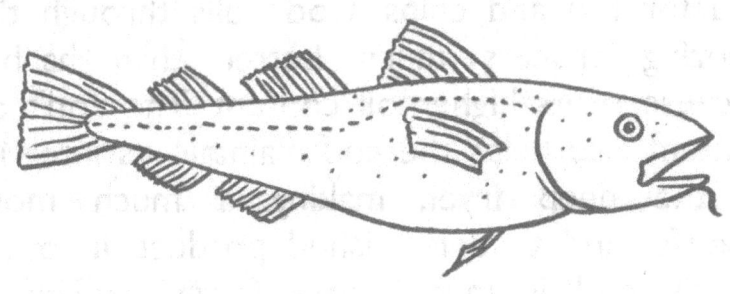

The Fish

I have a secret to confess. I grew so tired of using halibut for fish and chips that one of my sous chefs suggested to me, "Why don't you write this on the daily special menu—'Halibut Fish and Chips Made with Fresh Cod—Trust Me.'" You know what? It worked. Everyone ordered the fish and chips because it said halibut, and everyone also thought the fish that day was the most moist, flavorful, tender accompaniment to their chips! My point here is, halibut is phenomenal as a fresh fish, but it is not the best fish in a deep-fried application such as fish and chips.

Unfortunately, we have all been brainwashed to believe that because halibut is considered the cream of the crop, it should make the best fried fish too. But halibut is a very unforgiving fish: it easily overcooks, and subjecting it to the high heat of the deep fryer is one of the worst places for it. Please save your beautiful, fresh halibut for other cooking methods, and let's focus on fresh or frozen cod for fish and chips. Cod pulls through the freezing process much better than halibut because of its higher oil content. The cod's oil content also helps the cod maintain its integrity in the deep fryer, making a much more flavorful and tender finished product. In other words, cod is much more forgiving. This is why I recommend true cod, lingcod, or rockfish to make a superior fried fish. To be clear, fish that is marketed as ling cod is neither a ling nor a cod but a member of the greenling family and a voracious predator, to boot.

John Nelson's Fish & Chips Batter

Serves 4

2 cups all-purpose flour
1/4 teaspoon baking powder
Pinch of salt
12 ounces beer (play with different types of beer to find your favorite flavor)

The Coating:

2 cups rice flour
Pinch of salt
1/4 teaspoon white pepper
1/4 teaspoon granulated onion
1/4 teaspoon granulated garlic
Canola or peanut oil, for frying
2 pounds cod, cut into 3-inch portions

Let's be honest: to tell you everything I know about batters would require another book. So I'll just give you my personal favorite batter recipe. For a crisp, non-greasy fried fish on the outside, and a pure and tender inside, it's all about the coating. You'll see what I mean in the recipe that follows.

Of course, this is my personal bias, but I really don't like a greasy battered fish with my chips, do you?

There are many ways to create a light and crisp batter: soda water for lightness, baking powder for leavening and crispness, for example. But let's make it easy by whipping up a quick beer batter and making a crisp coating using seasoned rice flour, thus removing the worry of winding up with greasy fish.

Sift the flour, baking powder, and salt together in a mixing bowl. Mix in the beer with a wire whisk until smooth. Keep the batter in the refrigerator until ready to use.

Blend all coating ingredients together. Put the coating mix in a pie plate or other low dish.

Heat the frying oil to 375°F in a heavy-bottomed pot. Use enough oil to fill the pot only halfway, to guard against splash-over.

Dip fish in batter, scraping off excess batter against the side of the bowl to leave a light coating on the fish. Immediately dredge the battered fish in the coating mixture. Slowly place the fish in the hot oil and cook until it becomes a light golden brown.

Meanwhile, place a cooling rack on top of paper towels. Carefully remove the cooked fish from the hot oil with a slotted spoon. Place the fried fish on the rack to drain off excess oil. This method helps maintain a crispier end product versus putting the fish directly on a paper towel, which retains too much moisture and can lead to fish with soggy bottoms.

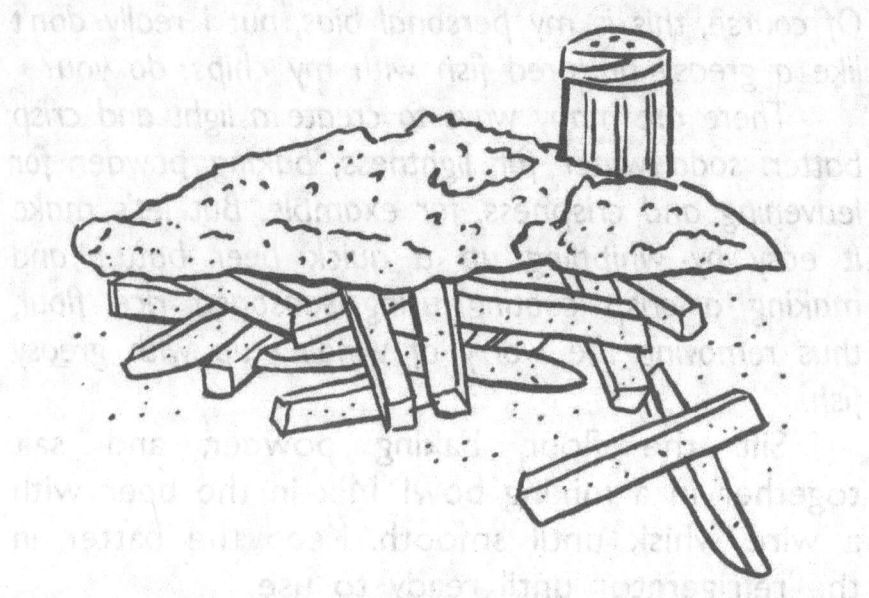

John's Grown-Up Fish Cakes

Serves 4

Fish cake mix:

1/2 teaspoon finely minced garlic
1 tablespoon grated onion
2 large bay leaves
1 tablespoon butter, plus more for frying
1 large egg, beaten
1 tablespoon heavy cream
1 teaspoon chopped fresh dill
Dash of allspice
Salt and white pepper
1 pound black cod, cod, or rockfish
1 boiled Russet potato, very soft, cooled

Fish cakes were a serious staple growing up. We'd eat them a few times every month, made out of salmon or whatever kind of fish we had. They're good at every meal and they make they make great sandwiches. There are many versions of this delicacy. This dish tastes best with a moist fish like black cod, regular cod, or rockfish. Fish cakes are often made with salt cod, but my recipe is made with fresh cod;

both ways are delicious. Serve them with a traditional tartar sauce and you'll know that life is good.

In a large pan, sauté the garlic, onion, and bay leaves in 1 tablespoon butter over medium heat until the onion becomes translucent. While the ingredients are sautéing, mix together the egg, cream, dill, allspice, and salt and pepper to taste in a medium bowl.

Add the fish to the sauté pan with the garlic and onion and continue cooking until the fish just begins to flake, and then remove the pan from the heat. Peel the potato and crumble it into the bowl with the egg mixture; gently stir until thoroughly mixed. Add the fish and other ingredients from the sauté pan (discarding the bay leaves), and gently stir, trying to keep the fish flaky. From this mixture, form tablespoon-size fish cakes and fry them in butter on medium heat until both sides of the cake are golden brown.

Fish Cakes Mom's Way

Serves 4

1 pound cod
2 tablespoons diced onion
1/4 cup cream
1 egg
3 tablespoons all-purpose flour or potato starch
Pinch of nutmeg
Pinch of allspice
1 teaspoon granulated garlic
1 teaspoon granulated onion
Salt and white pepper
Butter, for frying

My version of fish cakes is very traditional and chunkier than mom's version. She always made hers with raw ground fish and some flour or potato starch. I use a whole boiled potato. Mom's fish cakes are much more fine-textured and more tender than mine. I learned how to make fish cakes by watching Mom working at her chowder house—a little hole in the wall next to the cannery on the Ilwaco docks. I always loved the fish cakes, but my absolute favorites were the clam fritters and clam cakes. Pan-fried. I loved them. She always served all of her seafood cakes with a traditional tartar sauce, what else? *Both sides of my family are from Sweden, so you'll see the subtle Scandinavian touches of nutmeg and allspice in these. Yah, sure, you betcha—they're good.*

Using a food processor, blend the fish, onions, and cream until smooth. Add the egg and blend until incorporated. Add the flour, spices, and salt and pepper to taste and blend again. The mixture should be doughy but not thin. Form 4-inch cakes and fry them in butter on medium heat until both sides are golden brown.

Tea-Cured Black Cod

Serves 3

4 bags dark black tea
4 cups water
3/4 cup brown sugar
1/4 cup salt
1/4 teaspoon allspice
1/4 teaspoon cardamom
1 fillet of black cod, pin bones removed

Black cod, butterfish, or sablefish. Whatever you like to call it. The sablefish (its true name) is a fantastic rich, oily, and robust-flavored fish that is just perfect for curing. I like to use this recipe to smoke the sablefish.

Boil tea bags in the water until very strong and black. Remove from heat and add sugar, salt, allspice, and cardamom. Stir until sugar is dissolved. Refrigerate tea cure until completely cool.

Using a nonreactive pan or ziplock bag, pour tea cure over cod and place in refrigerator for a minimum of 4 hours; overnight is best. Once cured, remove and pat the fish dry. The cod is now ready to broil, barbeque, or panfry.

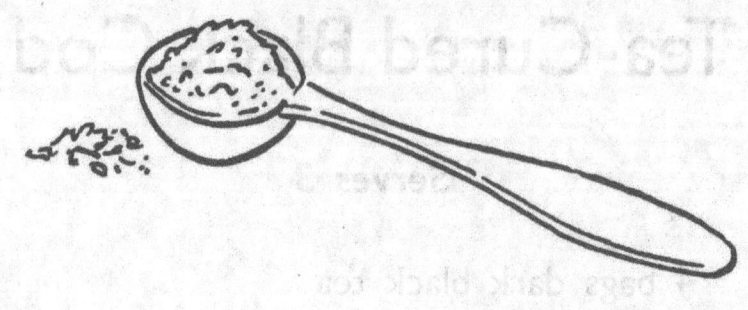

Fish Terrine

Serves 4

Fish cake mix, doubled
2 cups crawfish tail meat or small prawns (31 to 35 per pound)
1 tablespoon pickled beet juice
2 tablespoons chopped fresh dill
8 asparagus spears, blanched

I remember growing up in the Lutheran church with all the Swedes and, of course, doing the church basement suppers. They were great on the Pacific Northwest coast: everybody brought shrimp or crab off the boat or black cod or salmon something. I remember some awful aspic-type dishes, and I think this fish terrine is my antidote to those unpleasant concoctions.

This dish takes the fish cake recipe in another direction and turns it into a terrine, which is another word for a pâté—a well-seasoned ground meat or fish dish.

Line the bottom of a 4x9-inch loaf pan with parchment paper. Spray the bottom and sides with cooking spray.

Split the fish cake mix equally. Into one half, add the beet juice and mix well. Into the other half, add the chopped dill and mix well.

For the first layer, evenly spread the crawfish meat or shrimp on top of the parchment paper. For the second layer, evenly spread the fish cake mix with dill. On top of this layer, place the asparagus lengthwise, with a little space between spears. Now cover the asparagus with the fish cake mix colored with beet juice, spreading evenly on top.

Preheat the oven to 300°F. Bake the terrine uncovered for about 45 minutes, or until a toothpick inserted in the middle comes out clean.

The fish terrine may be served hot, cold, or at room temperature.

An Appetizer Terrine

For a tighter terrine, take another loaf pan of the same size and fill it with something heavy, like a couple of soup cans, and place it on top of the finished terrine and put the whole thing in the refrigerator overnight. Once chilled, unmold the terrine by running hot water around the outside bottom of the loaf pan, inverting it onto a cutting board, and tapping it. Serve the fish terrine with hardtack crackers, mustard, and **Marinated Cucumbers.**

Best Albacore Tuna for Sandwiches & Salad

Makes 6 to 8 sandwiches

1 to 1-1/2 pounds whole albacore tuna loin, cut into 2-inch-thick slices
2 small shallots, divided
1 inch-long piece fresh ginger, peeled and thinly sliced, divided
4 cloves garlic, divided
1/2 teaspoon kosher salt
1/2 teaspoon pepper
5 wide strips orange zest (from 1 orange; use a vegetable peeler)
6 large sprigs cilantro
3/4 cup salad oil
3/4 cup olive oil

Buying tuna in a can from the store is not something that was done. Each tuna season a small local canner was kept very busy canning thousands of cans of tuna for the tuna fisherman of the area, keeping the shelves stocked at home.

Place tuna slices on a baking sheet or cutting board.

Mince one shallot, half of the ginger, and 2 garlic cloves. Stir in the salt and pepper; mix and rub all over tuna slices. Place them in a 4x8-inch baking dish. Cover and chill for 4 to 5 hours.

Preheat oven to 275°F.

Quarter the remaining shallot lengthwise and add to baking dish with tuna in it. Crush remaining 2 garlic cloves and add to the dish, along with the orange zest, remaining ginger, and cilantro.

Blend olive oil and salad oil well; pour it in the dish to cover fish by 1/4 inch. Depending upon the size of tuna loin, you may need to make more or less of the oil blend.

Bake tuna for 30 minutes uncovered. Remove and refrigerate tuna in oil for up to five days.

Use this flavorful and tender tuna in place of store-bought canned tuna for amazing sandwiches and salads.

Tuna Gravlax with Radish & Cucumber

Serves 6 to 8

Tuna Gravlax:

- 2 tablespoons kosher salt
- 2 teaspoons sugar
- 1-1/2 pounds albacore tuna loin
- 4 sprigs fresh dill

Radish & Cucumber:

- 6 radishes, trimmed
- 1 small cucumber
- 2 to 3 tablespoons olive oil
- 1-1/2 teaspoons lemon juice
- 2 tablespoons chopped fresh chives
- 1/4 teaspoon sugar
- Salt

I love lox. There, I said it. I could eat gravlax everyday for every meal. But for a change, albacore tuna makes one of the cleanest-flavored lox that goes with just about everything you put it on.

For the gravlax: Combine salt and the sugar in a small bowl. Rub all sides of the tuna with this mixture. Lay dill underneath and on top of the tuna loin. Wrap tightly with plastic wrap. Set on a plate, and chill at least 6 hours and up to overnight.

Once the tuna has been the cured, briefly rinse fish with cold water and pat dry with paper towels. Using a very sharp knife, thinly slice tuna diagonally across the grain, pulling the knife through the fish rather than sawing. For paper-thin gravlax, place the sliced tuna on a plate, cover with plastic wrap and gently pound with the bottom of a 1-cup measuring cup until very thin.

For the radish and cucumber: Thinly slice radishes and cucumber, and cut into thin matchsticks. Transfer to a small bowl and add olive oil, lemon juice, chives, and sugar. Season with salt to taste and toss until well combined. Serve with the tuna gravlax.

Scattered Sushi Bowl with Seared Black Cod

Serves 4

The Rice:

1 cup raw short- to medium-grain rice (makes 3 cups cooked)
6 tablespoons rice vinegar
2 tablespoons sugar
2 teaspoons sake or mirin (sweet Japanese cooking wine)
2 teaspoons salt

The fish:

1 tablespoon peanut or canola oil
1-1/2-pound skinless black cod fillet

The Toppings:

Use any or all.
1-1/2 pounds cooked chanterelle mushrooms (sliced and sautéed in butter or olive oil until tender)

1/2 marinated cucumber, sliced
3 eggs, beaten and scramble cooked
1 cup snow peas, thinly sliced
1/2 sheet toasted nori (seaweed), very thinly sliced
3 tablespoons trout roe or tobiko (flying fish roe; wasabi tobiko is great for this recipe)
1 tablespoon toasted sesame seeds
Soy sauce (optional)
Wasabi (optional)
Thin slices of jalapeño or serrano chiles (optional)

This is a really simple dish, common in Asia. Make rice, and then scatter the ingredients on top. As a boy on the docks, I watched the men on the Japanese ships eating their rice bowls. The seared black cod makes it outrageously good. We need to eat more black cod, that's all I know. It's the Northwest version of Chilean sea bass—a little softer, but it has the same kind of rich, oily thing going on.

"Scatter sushi" is open to just about any ingredient you can think of, but I find the rich and tender black cod perfect for blending into the sushi rice and vegetables with chopsticks or a fork.

Cooking true "sushi rice" is an art. Pick up a book on the subject of rice cooking and prepare to be fascinated. For our purposes, though, let's make the rice as easy and tasty as possible.

Cook the rice following instructions on the package, or place the desired amount of rice in a heavy-bottomed saucepan and fill with cold water to about 1/2 inch above the rice. Bring rice to a boil, and then reduce the heat to a low simmer. Cover, but allow steam to escape slightly, and cook until all the water is gone and the rice is tender.

Mix all remaining ingredients together in a small bowl until the sugar and salt are no longer visible.

When the rice is cooked and tender, dump it into a large bowl, pour the vinegar mixture onto the rice, and gently blend it using two forks or large spoons, being careful not to smash the rice, which would make it mushy.

Coat a large sauté pan with the oil and get it hot. Sear the black cod until golden brown on each side and cooked through, about 1 minute per side. This will allow the meat to flake off so you can mix it easily in your bowl. Divide the 3 cups cooked rice among four bowls, and divide the fish among the bowls.

Add any or all of the other toppings to the bowls. Experiment and have fun! *Kampai* ("bottoms up," in Japanese)!

Photo from Shutterstock

A Dog & Crab Story

Holidays growing up were not about the hours spent laboring in the kitchen, worrying about the moistness of the turkey and the "whippiness" of the potatoes. No, it was all about how much crab you could shake and eat. Throw down the newspaper, scatter the Dungeness, and let the greed set in. If you weren't skilled at shaking the succulent meat from the shell, those who were more skilled at it would consume two, three, or sometimes four crabs to your half of one. Consequently, you could always tell the slow shakers—the half crab eaters—they were the ones in line for turkey and whipped potatoes.

December 1 is the traditional season opener for crab, so with the ability to dump the pots a week before, Thanksgiving slipped under the radar as the first crab feast of the season for us. I could always be found sitting by the pot of boiling saltwater that was surging with the pungent smell of pickling spices, talking with family and listening to Grandpa spin yarns about the Old Country in his thick Swedish accent. Activist relatives would be damning the dams on the Columbia River for what they did to the salmon runs, and others would be conversing about the latest storm to ravage the coast and how many crab pots would be lost.

One year, as I helped out with the crab boil, my yellow Lab, Duke, was beside me, sniffing the crabs awaiting the boil—and taunting fate. Noticing that the pot was empty, I reached down and picked out a couple jumbos to boil, when a sudden ear-splitting yelp came from my dog as he twirled frantically in circles, trying to hurl a vice-gripped crab from his bleeding nose. With a harsh yap, the gyrating Lab backed into another waiting crab, which had targeted his hind leg with both claws. Now my contorted yellow blur of a pooch had nowhere to run, with a crab stuck to his snout, and two on his hind leg, so he rolled like he was smothering a fire. The tenacious crabs, finally loosened by the crush of the rolling Duke, gave up their vicious grips. Duke knew he had just won the battle, and lay down next to the warm fire of the crab boil, licking his wounds. He looked at me as I picked up the prize-fighting crabs to throw them in the pot, and I sensed he felt a little respect. After all, they did get their last licks in before checking out in the hot salty water and pickling spice.

When it was time to chow down, I obsessed about whether to eat the sweet crabmeat as I shook it out, or to save it in a big pile to top a salad later. Hmmm ... always the chance of someone snatching it. I'd better eat it now.

I'd think about the only creatures that loved crab as much as I did; so much, in fact, that they would slip into the crab pots for a leisurely dining experience at the bottom of the sea. The octopus and wolf eel could possibly be the only ones to match my crab addiction. Unfortunately for them, they are also both delicious, and to this day I consume them whenever I get a chance—to help out the Dungeness population, you know.

I could write a whole book just on the subject of cooking Dungeness crab. How many ways can a crab be cooked? What is the best way to boil a crab? When is the crab finished boiling? Should I clean the crab before boiling? Should I cook the whole crab? How much and what is the best salt to use? Does a crab really make noise when plunged into boiling water? Is the crab done when it turns red? Is the crab best hot or chilled? These are a few of the mysteries and more we will explore. Here are the basics.

Traditional Boiled Crab

Serves 4

Bring enough water to boil to completely cover 4 crabs. Use 1 cup kosher salt per quart of water; absolutely no iodized table salt.

When the water is at a full rolling boil, add the crabs whole and return to boil. Cook crabs for 20 minutes from immersion. Remove crabs, clean, and eat the crabmeat warm.

If the crab is to be used later, plunge hot crab into ice-cold salted water (same proportion as above). Remove when chilled and refrigerate.

Should you clean a crab before you cook it? My cousin Myrtle would have shuddered if you didn't clean the crab before cooking, and Myrt was married to a prominent crabber and tuna fisherman. So if that is your preference, by all means, tidy your crab up before plunging it into the boiling pot. But for a foodie like me, you are missing all the goodies inside the shell—sorry, Myrt. A crab is really a meal in a shell—between the "butter," the new shell growing "poor man's lobster," the heart, and the nectar, you definitely have a complete flavor explosion ready for dressings, topping your rice, and more.

What is the best way to cook a crab? Well, this depends on how you are serving it. If you are leaning towards an Asian flair, clean the crab, break it in sections, and sauté it in chili and fermented black bean, for example.

For boiling the crab to achieve the best flavor, use seawater and kelp. The salinity of the seawater is the perfect ratio. But most of us may not be able to just run to the beach and scoop a bucket of seawater and pluck kelp. My best recommendation, and how I prepare my boiled crab, is as follows:

Using the salt ratio of 1 cup kosher salt to 1 quart of water, also add to your water 1/2 cup pickling spice for every four crabs and 2 large leaves of kombu seaweed (found in most Asian stores) for every four crabs; follow the directions and time for **boiling a crab.**

Is the crab done when it turns red? This is not a good way to tell when the crab is done. Crabs turn red almost immediately when plunged into boiling water, so you would have to be adept at knowing the degree of the red shade to know when it is done. There is one little trick that works well, in case you lose track of time while imbibing. Generally, when a crab is done, it loses some of its nectar and butter and this floats to the surface, creating a foam-like froth on the top of the boiling water. When this happens, you can be sure this is a pretty good time to pull your crab.

Is the crab best hot or cold? Served either way is delicious. But remember this: cook it once unless you're making crab cakes. In other words, if you cook some for later and chill it, then you want to serve it chilled rather than reheating it.

Does a crab make a noise when plunged in boiling water? *The only noise that you hear will be "when will they be done?"*

"Fifteen minutes ... great! There's time for another cold beer!"

Dungeness Crab Cakes

Serves 4 to 6

3/4 cup good-quality mayonnaise
1 scant tablespoon Dijon mustard
1 tablespoon lemon juice
1 teaspoon horseradish
Couple of splashes hot sauce, or more if you like
1 large egg
3 tablespoons all-purpose flour
1/2 teaspoon baking powder
3/4 cup cracker meal
1/2 teaspoon freshly ground black pepper
1 tablespoon chopped flat-leaf parsley
2 green onions, thinly sliced
2 pounds crabmeat
Butter, for frying

It's not just the ingredients but how you use them. Let's put them together right to make a great cake!

Whisk mayonnaise with all the wet ingredients until creamy smooth. Whisk flour, baking powder, cracker meal, and pepper with your wet ingredients until completely blended.

Add parsley and green onion and blend into wet mixture.

Fold in the crabmeat gently as to not break into small pieces; you want to have big chunks for great texture in your cakes. If your mixture seems a bit wet, wait for at least 5 minutes for the cracker meal to fully absorb the moisture. If the mixture still seems a bit too loose, don't add more cracker, but dust the top of the mixture with a bit more flour and carefully fold it in.

Fry the crab cakes in butter on moderate heat until golden brown on both sides. A good cake should be golden outside and just a touch underdone on the inside; it should be just a bit moist in the middle rather than dry all the way through.

Crab Butter Vinaigrette

Makes 1-1/4 cups

1/4 cups
1/4 cup rice vinegar
1 teaspoon Dijon mustard
1 tablespoon crab butter
Pinch of kosher or sea salt
1 teaspoon lemon juice
Pinch of cayenne pepper
1 cup extra virgin olive oil

I try to use every edible part of the crab, including the liquid called "butter." After trying this recipe for salad vinaigrette, you'll be glad you looked for and saved the butter before tossing out your crab waste. A rich-yellow crab butter has the best flavor.

Whisk all ingredients, except oil, thoroughly. Blend oil in slowly to create an emulsion.

Serve on a crisp salad with **Salmon Chicharrones.**

Crab Shell Rice

Serves 2

1/4 cup finely minced red onion
1 teaspoon finely minced ginger
2 cloves garlic, minced
1/2 cup finely chopped cabbage
Vegetable oil, for sautéing
2 tablespoons sweet chili sauce
1 tablespoon fish sauce
1 tablespoon soy sauce
2 tablespoons sake
4 cups day-old cooked rice
Freshly ground black pepper
Crab butter, nectar, and soft shell
2 whole crab shells

Not only is there a meal under the shell of the crab, but there are other goodies that you can save when cleaning your crab—the butter, nectar (the yellow liquid stuff), and soft shell. Save it all in the shell of the crab for this simple recipe that packs a lot of flavor.

Sauté the onion, ginger, garlic, and cabbage in oil until tender. Add the sweet chili, fish, soy sauce, and sake, and let it come to a simmer. Add the rice and sauté until most of the liquid is absorbed. Put your rice mixture into a bowl.

Add the crab butter, nectar, and soft shell to the rice and toss. Fill the two shells with the rice mixture. Lightly cover with foil. Bake at 325°F for 25 to 30 minutes. Remove foil and bake for 5 minutes more. Serve in the shell.

Pacific Popcorn Shrimp

Serves 5

1 pound of Pacific pink shrimp, fresh or thawed and drained well
Splash of rice vinegar
1 large egg yolk
1/4 teaspoon cayenne pepper
1 teaspoon granulated garlic
1 teaspoon granulated onion
1/2 teaspoon ground celery seed
1 teaspoon salt
2 cups cracker meal
1 cup rice flour
Oil, for frying

The small size of the sweet Pacific pink shrimp is perfect for this addicting anytime snack. I remember from my childhood the sweet smell of cooking shrimp rolling from the steam vents of the ancient cannery standing defiantly on thick wooden piers over the waters of the Columbia. The best snack was grabbing a small plastic bag of warm shell-on shrimp straight off the line and popping them in my mouth, shell and all. I prefer this recipe with shell-on pink shrimp, but most readily available is fresh or frozen shell-off.

Lie the drained shrimp on a sheet pan and blot dry with paper towels. Wipe the sheet pan dry; it will be used for the coated shrimp before cooking.

In a mixing bowl, whisk the vinegar with the egg yolk until completely blended and just a touch frothy. Mix all the dry ingredients and have ready to pour into the bowl. Add shrimp to the egg yolk mixture and toss. Pour shrimp and egg yolk through a strainer; you want just enough egg yolk to barely coat the shrimp. Rinse and dry the mixing bowl and add all mixed dry ingredients. Slowly add shrimp to the dry mixture and toss a small amount at a time so each shrimp is thoroughly coated.

Add oil to a 3- to 5-quart saucepan until half full. Heat oil to 350°F. Add small amounts of shrimp to the oil, being careful not to splash. Fry in small batches while slowly moving the shrimp around so they don't stick to each other; remove when golden brown and drain on paper plates or towels.

Spot Roe Caviar with Miso

Makes about 1 cup

Roe of 15 to 20 fresh spot prawns

One of the great things about our spot prawns from the cold Pacific, besides their sweet, rich flavor, is the amount of roe they produce. If you have ever bought a bag of fresh spots, you know what I am talking about—all that red roe nestled underneath the tail is just waiting to be made into caviar! Here is the simple process for making your own:

Using your thumb, scrape the roe from the underside of the tail in to a bowl.

Add enough cold fresh water to the bowl just to cover but not float the roe. With clean hands or a rubber spatula, whisk the roe vigorously to break the eggs from the membranes.

In another bowl, prepare the salt solution by mixing 1 heaping tablespoon kosher or sea salt and 2 tablespoons yellow miso to 3 cups cold water, and stir to dissolve.

Using a cheesecloth-lined strainer, strain the eggs from the water and remove any membrane that may be visible. Bundle up the cheesecloth and lift from the strainer. Gently immerse the cheesecloth with the eggs into the salt solution. Open the bundle and let the eggs wash out into the solution, once again watching for and removing any membrane. Let the eggs cure for a minimum of 6 hours in the refrigerator. After the eggs have cured, strain and pack in a nonreactive glass container.

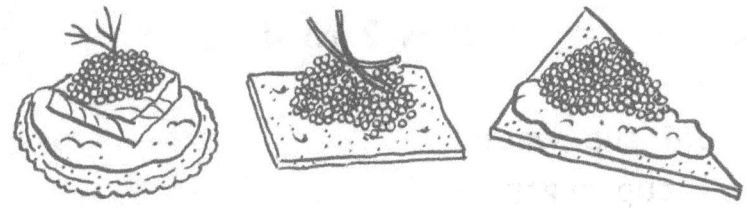

Seared Scallops with Dill & Sugar-Soaked Lemon Salsa

Serves 2 to 4

3/4 cup water
1 cup sugar
1 lemon, sliced into 1/4-inch rounds

For the Lemon Salsa:

1 tablespoon toasted pine nuts
1 tablespoon sliced seedless red grapes
1/4 teaspoon crushed red chili flakes
2 teaspoons reserved lemon simple syrup (from the soaking lemons)
1 teaspoon chopped fresh dill
1 teaspoon rice vinegar
Pinch of salt
12 large (under 10 per pound) fresh dry-packed scallops
Butter, for searing

When buying scallops, ask for dry-packed scallops for the closest thing to real, out-of-the-shell scallops. Plan one day ahead for this dish so the lemons can soak properly. Trust me, it's worth it.

Combine water and sugar in a saucepan and bring to a simmer to create a simple syrup. Once all the sugar has melted, add lemon slices and immediately refrigerate for at least 8 hours.

After 8 hours, remove lemons and dice small. Combine diced lemons, pine nuts, grapes, chili flakes, lemon syrup, dill, vinegar, and salt and mix gently.

Using a paper towel, pat the scallops dry. On medium-high heat, melt just enough butter to coat the pan; cook until brown then add scallops. Fry until golden brown on each side.

Plate scallops with Lemon Salsa and enjoy.

Crab Cocktail with Crab Butter & Radish

Makes about 2 cups

3 large red radishes, finely diced
1 green onion, finely chopped
1 teaspoon finely chopped fresh dill
2 tablespoons **Crab Butter Vinaigrette**
1 pound crabmeat

This recipe is a great twist on the traditional cocktail. Here we use the fat, or butter, of the crab to make this "cocktail sauce" and the radish for the horseradish kick.

Very simply mix all ingredients except crabmeat with the Crab Butter Vinaigrette; then gently fold in the crab serve with hardtack crackers.

Photo from Shutterstock

Sole & Rockfish

The One-Eyed Pirate

At first glance, you would have thought him a wild-eyed pirate lacking the patch but not the missing eye. The missing eye was replaced with a glass facsimile not completely in fit with the other eye, giving the appearance of too many snorts of Everclear and a few too many hits to the head by the flopper stoppers. Densmoore not only trusted the saltwater in his veins to see him through but also put full faith in the cement hull of his dragger to see him safely across the wild seas. My stepfather was his deckhand, and I met them regularly when they came in to deliver ground fish to the processing plant.

I will always recall one muggy, overcast day standing on the delivery dock perched above the mighty Columbia River at full ebb. Putting the bow of the cement-hulled *Resolute* into the powerful current, the pirate haphazardly but efficiently worked the throttle of the now groaning boat close enough to the dock to throw the mooring lines. The diesel engine belched black smoke from its stack as Densmoore put the coals to her to match the power of the outgoing tide and keep her steady while my stepfather threw the lines up to me to tie off on the cleats, first the bow and then the stern.

After the engine was shut down, I worked my way down the slippery wooden ladder to the deck of the boat, wondering what would happen if I fell into the green water below, which was making the dock pilings wiggle and vibrate from the fierce power of the now full ebb. With both feet off the slippery ladder, I carefully crossed the slick deck and peered into the hold, looking down to see my stepfather, Geno, surrounded by a pretty skookum catch of mostly Petrale sole, some Dover, and much rockfish.

"Come on down and give me a hand, boy," he groused in a stormy, seagoing voice. I happily agreed and worked my way down the scaly ladder, realizing there was no smell on earth like climbing down into a fish hold smelling of fresh fish, saltwater, and the diesel stench from the bilge.

I was standing in the money pit—the hold—admiring all the different bottom fish when the cannery worker above gave the warning that he was lowering the bucket down for us to fill with fish. Once the bank safe–sized bucket lay on the bottom of the hold, Geno and I used shovel and hand to fill it brimming with the last few days' catch. "No, no! Just Petrale in this one," Geno would say, as I accidentally grabbed a Dover. When all the flatfish were gone, we moved to the rockfish and cod. Black rock, red rock, brown rock, lingcod, true cod, all pitched into the bucket for the last haul up by the hoist to the processing plant.

Climbing the fish scale ladder back out of the hold, I heard the diesel engine roar back to life with a black smoke belch. Geno scurried up the ladder to the top of the dock as the pirate shouted out from the wheelhouse, "Cast off the lines, Geno. We're heading up the river for fuel." *Well, I guess it's just me and the pirate,* I thought, as the lines hit the metal deck and Geno waved good-bye.

As the gray overcast clouds gave way to the sinking sun of the late afternoon and the tumultuous ebb tide settled into slack tide, I made my way into the wheelhouse, where the pirate sat nudging the throttle and slipping the cement boat away from the dock and into the now calm channel of the mighty Columbia. I stood next to the wild-eyed pirate, who had one eye on the direction of the boat and the other staring at the floor as we ran east up the river. Looking forward out the cracked windows of the wheelhouse, I could see the Astoria Bridge, four miles long and tall enough to let the largest of ships pass under, defiantly standing a half mile away. You know the one: remember Number Five from *Short Circuit* jumping off the top?

"Hey, I need to go below. Watch the wheel," snarled Densmoore.

"Sure, no problem," I said, as I slowly and cautiously sat in the captain's chair feeling like I had just been given the controls to the *Apollo* rocket.

As I basked in my newfound glory at the wheel, I heard the pirate bellow like a broken pipe organ from below, "Don't touch the wheel!"

Uh, you just told me to watch the wheel. Besides, we are heading for the base of the bridge. "Don't touch the wheel? I hope you can turn her from below!"

"Don't touch the wheel!"

"Okay..." I weakly said, as I watched in terror from the captain's chair while the huge footing of the Astoria Bridge came closer and closer to the bow of the boat. Just as I was ready to crank her hard to starboard, the pirate came busting from below, barking at me why I wasn't watching the wheel and crank her over fast before we take down the four-mile-long bridge and sink like a cement boat. Quickly I yanked her to starboard, and with the boat back in the channel and my heart back on pace, the wild pirate turns and grins at me with teeth in need of an Ospho treatment and one eye looking to port and the other staring at me said only, "Good one." Damn crazy pirate humor, I thought.

Poached Petrale Sole with Shrimp Filling

Serves 2

Water
1 bottle white wine
4 bay leaves
6 whole cloves
1 clove garlic, smashed
Salt and pepper
2 cups fresh Pacific pink shrimp, peeled, deveined, and tails removed, divided
1 teaspoon fresh lemon juice
1 teaspoon Dijon mustard
Couple dashes of Tabasco sauce
1 large egg
1-1/2 teaspoons finely minced green onion
1/2 cup finely ground day-old hearty bread
1 teaspoon finely minced fresh dill
4 fresh Petrale sole fillets

My mom had a restaurant on the mouth of the Columbia River, and one the most popular dishes was Sole Joanna, her rendition of sole stuffed with Pacific pink shrimp. You may use other types of sole, such as Dover, but the firmness of the Petrale is best for this recipe.

For the poaching liquid, in a 4-inch-deep stovetop pan, add half water and half white wine (no oak, please) to fill pan halfway up. Add the bay leaves, cloves, and garlic. Add a touch of salt and pepper.

In a mixing bowl, add 1 cup of the shrimp, lemon, mustard, and Tabasco; with the back of a fork or wide spoon, coarsely mash these ingredients. Now mix in the egg, onion, bread crumbs, and dill until completely incorporated. Add the rest of the shrimp and carefully mix in, not breaking them up.

While the poaching stock is coming to a very low simmer, lay each fillet out with the clear white flesh-side down, because that is the presentation side.

Divide your shrimp mixture among the 4 fillets. Spread mixture evenly down the center of the fillets and roll them up, not too tightly, starting at the tail end. Gently place fillets in poaching stock and cover with a lid. The fillets should be submerged half to three-quarters of the way. Once again, the stock should be at a very low simmer, not boiling. Simmer the fillets, covered, for approximately 8 to 12 minutes, depending on their size. To check for doneness, insert a thin knife into the center of the fillet; let the knife stand for a couple of seconds. Remove the knife and feel the tip: if the knife is piping hot, your fish is ready to go.

Whole Crispy Fried RockFish with Fennel & Cabbage

Serves 4

The Fish:

2-1/2 pounds whole rockfish or surfperch, gutted, gilled, and scaled
2 cups Ponzu
Frying oil, for filling half of a heavy-bottomed pot.
Cornstarch, for liberally dredging each fish

Fennel and Cabbage:

1 small head Napa cabbage, sliced thinly crosswise
1-1/2 teaspoons kosher or sea salt
1-1/2 tablespoons oil from frying the fish, cleared of debris
2 small dried chiles, roughly chopped (Thai or Serrano)
1 clove garlic, thinly sliced

1 small bulb fennel, thinly shaved
Zest of 1/2 lemon
1 tablespoon lemon juice
1/4 cup mirin
2 small splashes fish sauce
2 teaspoons sugar

The world over, fish is prepared whole. Fortunately for us in the Northwest, we have some of the best cold-water saltwater fish for this type of preparation. Why cook the fish whole? The answer is very simple—flavor, flavor, flavor. Anytime you can cook something on the bone and skin on, the moisture and flavor are tremendously enhanced.

Choose a heavy-bottomed pot large enough to hold 1 fish at a time.

Remove the dorsal spines from each fish with a knife or scissors.

Score the fish by making cuts from the top of the fish all the way to the belly at a slight front-to-back angle. Score in about 1-inch to 1-1/2-inch sections down to the backbone.

Set the fish in a high-sided dish and douse the scores with Ponzu, working the sauce into the scored meat. Let stand for at least 30 minutes.

Heat the oil to 325°F. Remove fish from the sauce and pat dry. Very liberally dredge one fish with cornstarch. Very slowly lower the fish into the hot oil and completely submerge. Fry for approximately 5 minutes for a 1-pound fish; 7 minutes for a 2-pound fish.

To check for doneness, lift fish from the oil with a slotted spatula or spider and, with a fork, try to lift one of the scored sections from the backbone. If the scored section lifts easily from the bone, it is ready. Transfer to paper towels set over a rack to drain. Repeat for other fish.

Fennel and Cabbage:

A wok works well for this recipe.

Place the sliced cabbage and salt in a nonreactive bowl and toss well; let stand for 15 minutes.

Heat the oil over medium heat. Add chiles to the oil and fry until they start to toast, or lose a bit of their color. Add the garlic and fry lightly.

Just as the garlic starts to brown, add cabbage, squeezing moisture out of it into the bowl before placing it in the chile-garlic oil. Fry cabbage just until it starts to wilt; then add fennel, lemon zest, lemon juice, mirin, fish sauce, and sugar. Fry for 30 seconds more while stirring all ingredients well.

Plate the fried fish by pulling off any pointy or sharp dorsal or pectoral fins that may remain. Leave the tail on for sure, because the tips are generally crisp and tasty! Ladle warm cabbage over the fish and serve. The idea is to pop off the scored section of fish with a bit of the cabbage and enjoy!

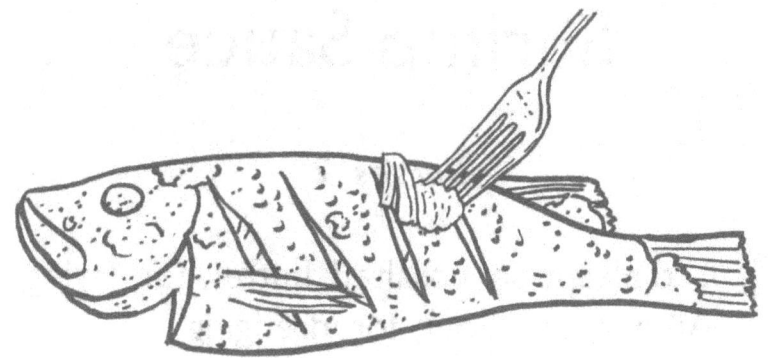

Golden Fried Sole with Shrimp Sauce

Serves 2

1 tablespoon unsalted butter, for frying
All-purpose flour, for dredging
3 eggs
Salt and pepper
4 sole fillets

Shrimp Sauce:

1 shallot, chopped
1 small clove garlic, thinly sliced
1/2 tablespoon unsalted butter for sautéing
3 tablespoons vodka
1 cup heavy cream
1/4 cup fresh Pacific pink shrimp, peeled, deveined, and tails removed
Juice of 1 lemon
Chopped fresh dill, for garnish
Marinated Cucumbers, for garnish

This technique is particularly useful for the softer Dover sole but delicious on any sole.

Set the butter to melt in a skillet on medium heat.

Put flour on a plate. In a low-sided bowl or pan, beat the eggs and season with salt and pepper to taste.

Simply dredge the fillets in flour first, dip them in the egg, and move them to the skillet. Fry in butter until golden on each side.

Sauté the shallot and garlic in butter until translucent. Remove pan from the heat and add the vodka; then return to the heat and cook vodka until it is reduce by a third. Add cream and simmer until reduced by half. Now add the fresh shrimp and lemon juice to finish.

Plate the golden fried fillets of sole with shrimp sauce on top and garnish with dill and **Marinated Cucumbers.**

Poached Rockfish Fillet with Wild Mushrooms

Serves 2 to 4

1-1/2 tablespoons butter
3 bay leaves
1 cup dried wild mushrooms
Pinch of salt and pepper
1 small shallot, minced
1 cup sweet white wine
3 cups water
Juice of 1/2 lemon
1 large clove garlic, thinly sliced
2 tablespoons white wine Worcestershire sauce
4 thick rockfish fillets, pin bones removed

With its many different varieties, the catchall rockfish it is one of my favorite fish. Depending upon species of rockfish, the fillets can vary from firm to delicate with a great flaky texture. Generally rockfish is marketed as snapper, which is a misnomer. Wild mushroom is a great complementary ingredient to these flavor-accepting fillets.

Add butter to a sauté pan over moderate heat. Add bay leaves, dried mushrooms, salt and pepper to taste, and shallot, and sauté until shallot is soft. Add wine and cook for 30 seconds more, and then add water, lemon juice, garlic, and Worcestershire sauce. Bring to a simmer and cover until mushrooms become tender. While stock is at a simmer, add fillets of rockfish. Poach until they yield to your touch but don't flake apart.

Serve in a deep dish with some of the mushrooms and stock spooned over the top.

Rockfish Hash

Serves 2

3 to 4 leftover baked or boiled potatoes, diced with skins on
1/2 red onion, thinly sliced lengthwise
1/2 small bulb fennel, thinly sliced
1 large clove garlic, minced
1/2 teaspoon pickling spice, finely ground in a spice grinder
Salt and pepper
2 tablespoons unsalted butter, for frying
2 rockfish fillets, cut into 1-inch cubes

Corned beef hash will never seem the same after you try this delicious version of the classic. Oh, and it's not just for breakfast anymore!

In a mixing bowl, mix together all ingredients except the butter and fish. Fry all ingredients in the unsalted butter until the fennel and onion become soft. Add fish and continue to fry until potatoes brown.

Serve with poached eggs for a great breakfast, lunch, or dinner.

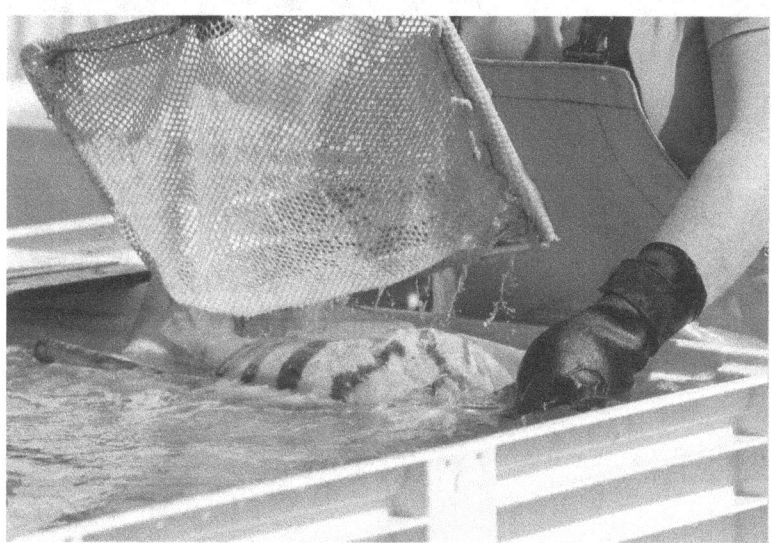

Photo from Shutterstock

Photo from Shutterstock

Bad Clam Karma

"You boys been digging a little too much?"

"No sir," I said to the warden, as the sound of crunching shells came from my hip boots with every step. Having forgotten my commercial fishing license at home, I had dug just a few too many razor clams for the sport digging limit and stuffed the excess in my boots in hopes of making it to my truck 100 yards away without getting caught. I know you're thinking waste, waste, waste. If I were skinnier, I would give that to you, but let's just say the clams did not go unused.

"Let's have a look at what you got," the warden said, peering into our nets. As I gave him my clam bag, I could feel the extra clams in my boots starting to become chowder between my toes, and the broken shells were slashing my shins. The warden spread the clams out on the hard sand, admiring the size and condition. "You boys digging commercially?" My buddy had his commercial fishing license and spoke up, "Yes, we are!" "Okay then," said the warden. "See you around next time," and he strolled down the sun-soaked beach.

After gathering our clams back up, I was too paranoid to empty my boots, so we began the walk back to the truck. It must have been Clam Killer Karma, because on the way to our wheels, we came across two bikini-clad blondes digging in the sand. As I tried to slip by them unnoticed, with hip boots full of clam fritters, the two girls bounced toward us and asked how we got the clams, because all they found were a bunch of holes.

Why now? Why not when I was playing football on the beach, or having a bonfire—why was this opportunity to meet the girls of my adolescent dreams happening while I was sloshing in clam goo? Bad Clam Karma, that's why. Well, my buddy and I made the best of the situation and were all too eager to give pointers, and then stand back to watch as they attacked sand shrimp holes that they erroneously thought were razor clam holes. "You're doing a great job, girls." "Gee, I can't imagine why they're getting away so fast. Keep digging, you'll find them," I said. Leaning on my clam shovel, with legs stiff as driftwood, trying not to move and give away the secret in my hip boots, I thought, "I hope there's no such thing as Bad Bikini Karma!"

Mussels with Slab Bacon & Star Anise

Serves 2

2 pounds fresh mussels, beards removed
1 cup diced slab bacon (1/2-inch cubes)
3 star anise
1 clove garlic, finely minced
2 small green onions, thinly sliced
1/2 tablespoon fresh lemon juice
2 tablespoons sweet white wine (Riesling)
1 tablespoon butter

Using a sauté pan over medium heat, cook the bacon until crisp.

Add to the crisp bacon the star anise, garlic, and green onions; cook until the aroma of the star anise is pungent.

Add the white wine and mussels and sauté until the shells pop.

Once the shells pop, finish with lemon and butter.

Sesame-Studded & Flash-Fried Razor Clams

Serves 2

6 to 8 razor clams
1 cup cracker meal
1/2 cup all-purpose flour
Salt and pepper
2 tablespoons black sesame seeds
2 eggs
Oil, for frying

There is a theory for cooking seafood such as razor clams, squid, etc.: cook it either 30 seconds or 30 minutes to keep it tender. Anything in between will render something suitable for a shoe. Hot and fast is the best for your razors.

Remove clams from their shells and rinse out any sand.

Mix all dry ingredients thoroughly in one bowl. In another bowl, beat the eggs with a touch of water.

First, dip razors in egg. Next, dredge razors in the mixed dry ingredients, making sure you lay razors flat with the digger open.

Pour oil into a frying pan to cover the bottom completely. Heat just until the smoking

point. Fry clams quickly, just until the coating becomes golden brown on each side.
Remove from pan immediately and serve.

Chopped Razor Ceviche Served in the Shell

Serves 4

4 razor clams, coarsely diced
2 green onions, finely chopped, white included
1 clove garlic, finely minced
1 tablespoon finely chopped dill
1/2 tablespoon finely chopped watercress
Juice of 1 lime
2 inches celery rib, finely chopped
1 teaspoon rice vinegar
2 teaspoons sugar
1 teaspoon chili flakes

Sometimes neither 30 seconds nor 30 minutes will do for the desirable razor clam. Chopped raw and "cooked" with citrus is the most pure in flavor and tender in texture, next to pulling it straight from the beach.

To remove the razor clam meat from the shell, bring a pot of water to a strong boil and plunge the clams very quickly into the boiling water just until the shell pops. Then immediately immerse in ice water to cool. Remove the clams from the shells and clean them *(see instruction)*. Save the shells.

Chop clams coarsely. Mix all remaining ingredients and toss with the chopped clam meat. Allow the mixture to stand for about 15 minutes in the refrigerator before serving. Serve in the shell of the clam.

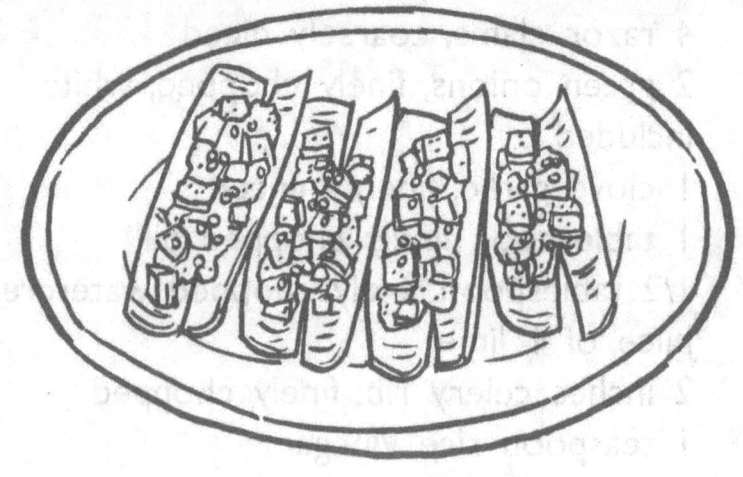

Sea Urchin Soup-Bowl Style

Serves 3

3 sea urchins
1 fennel bulb, green removed
1 tablespoon butter
2 cloves garlic, minced
1 cup diced onion
2 bay leaves
1/4 cup anisette
1/4 cup dry white wine
4 cups clam juice
1 cup heavy cream
Salt and white pepper
1/2 lemon

Rich and decadent is one way to describe the luxurious flavor of sea urchin. I like to say the flavor of the urchin is like the taste of the ocean wrapped in a creamy butterscotch candy. Maybe not eloquent but, oh, so good.

Clean the sea urchin using this **technique.** Rinse the sea urchin roe very gently with water; and save the bottom portion of the shell and clean well.

Slice fennel bulb lengthwise, then slice thinly across the grain.

In a heavy-bottomed soup pot on moderate heat, heat the butter and sauté the garlic, onion, and fennel until fennel becomes tender. Reduce heat and add bay leaves, anisette, and wine; reduce by half. Add clam juice and heavy cream. Purée 2 of the urchin roe and whisk into the soup and let simmer. Season with salt and pepper to taste.

Using the sea urchin shells as the bowls, ladle enough soup to fill each shell three-quarters full. Place the remaining roe in the soup, squeeze a little lemon juice on top, and serve.

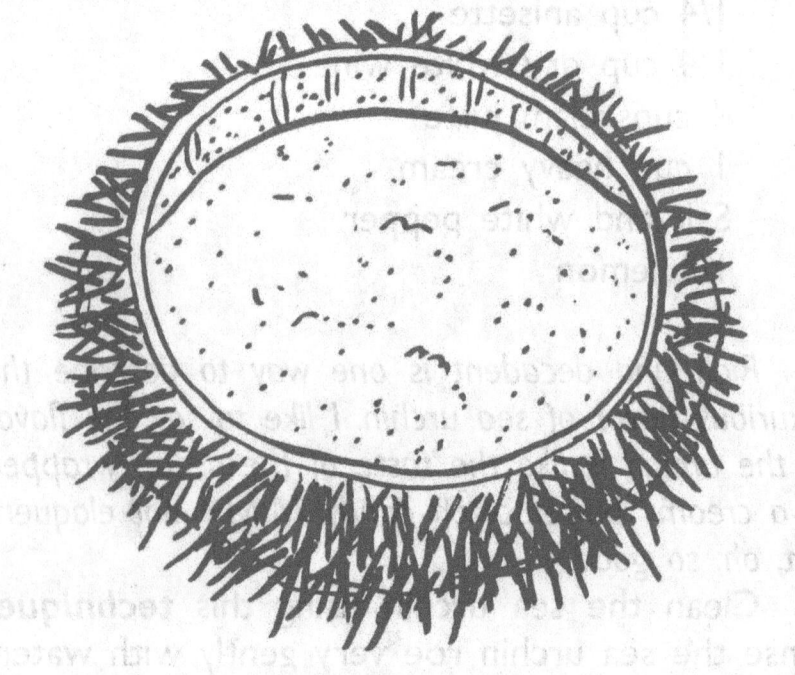

Photo from Shutterstock

Photo from Shutterstock

Oyster Bonfires & Daydreams

Near the mouth of the Columbia River next to the jetty of the Chinook mooring basin stretches a white sandy beach. Many family oyster bonfires and crab feeds took place here, as the commercial boats passed by as they went in and out of the harbor to deliver or harvest their catch. This beach held a kind of magic that would wash up on its shore. You see, hidden in the small pebbles scattered on the white sand are treasures such as Indian beads, fine porcelain from shipwrecks, and jellyfish the size of a basketball cut in half. While the family bonfire was being fired up, I would scour the beach for these treasures and dream of their stories, like a piece of porcelain worn by the years of running with the tides. The ornate blue pattern of the broken piece must have been from a special dinner plate, a plate for the captain of a tall sailing ship exploring the dangerous waters of the North Pacific. Not a plate for the lowly crew, this must have been the plate used by the courageous, sword-wielding, one-eyed captain at the helm of the ship, dressed smartly and cursing the storm bearing down on him and his crew! I could hear him bellowing orders over the gale-force wind-driven rain. "The gale will wreck us, men. Drop the canvas to the deck!"

"Captain, there be rocks dead off the bow!" screamed a scurvy-looking first mate. "Keep the foresail high! Let the rest of the canvas drop," the captain yelled over the screeching howl of the wind.

It was too late; all of the sails were lying on the deck in crumpled heaps, and with no way to swing the bow away from the rocks, the ship slammed into the boulders of the north shore of the Columbia River, ripping her to pieces. As the crew jumped in desperation, the captain gallantly clung to the wheel, wielding his sword in defiance of the storm. The black sea now began to take over his spirit, and with his last breath he could smell the saltwater, seaweed, and ... oysters?

"Hey, John, the oysters are ready!" yelled Uncle Lonny. Snapping back to reality, I pocketed the piece of porcelain and ran back to the bonfire, where in the simmering coals nestled a couple dozen oysters just beginning to pop and give up their succulent meat. All of the family gathered around the fire and picked out the perfect oysters and popped the top shell off the rest of the way with a knife. With a dash of hot sauce, a squeeze of lemon, or a drop of butter, we all scooped out the tender oysters and ate until we could eat no more.

Feeling a little sleepy, I laid back against a piece of driftwood with my feet buried in the sand, watching the sun go down over the river. The briny flavor still on my tongue and the smell of saltwater and seaweed creeping up the beach from the outgoing tide reminded me of the smartly dressed, sword-wielding, one-eyed captain. I wondered if he ate oysters off of the piece of broken porcelain plate I was rubbing between my fingers. I bet he did.

The Art of the Oyster

Ah, the oyster—that much misunderstood bivalve of the seas and bays of this planet. Known for its aphrodisiacal reputation, yet it lives alone, having no contact with its own species. But don't feel too sorry for this tasty little morsel. You see, I believe some things are on this earth to bring joy and pleasure to our senses, such as a beautiful flower for the eyes, the touch of a lover, or the taste sensation of an oyster. The oyster is a one-of-a-kind sensory stimulus; there is no other thing on earth that is so willing to gather and store the flavors of its surroundings in a wonderfully creamy interior surrounded by a neat protective shell just waiting for you to pop it open and marvel at all the possible ways

> to consume it. So, hail to the oyster for its unselfish life devoted to our eating pleasure!

Barbequed Oysters on the Grill or Fire Pit

> Really simple to do but the results are pure. Here are a couple of twists on the traditional. A recipe is really not needed for this preparation, just an explanation of how fun it is to throw an oyster au natural on the heat and pop it.
> The beer is chilled and the coals are hot. Whether you are in your backyard with the barbeque at your side, or on the beach with your toes in the sand and the coals of the bonfire glowing like the setting sun, a barbequed oyster is as close to bivalve nirvana as you might experience.
> The trick is to place the oyster over or beside the heat. In other words, an indirect heat is best—hot enough to penetrate the shell but not so hot that it burns the meat. Watch your oyster closely. Once the shell begins to

pop or the nectar begins to bubble between the two shells, remove immediately.

From here it is up to you: pop open the shell the rest of the way and devour, or pop open the shell just enough to add a bit of butter, beer, hot sauce, garlic, soy, sweet chili sauce, or whatever is your seasoning of choice. Then push the shell back together, place the oyster back on the indirect heat for another minute or so, then remove, open, and enjoy.

For some fun, stuff the partially opened shell with your favorite salsa or chopped bacon and put it back on the fire. The possibilities are endless for enhancing that plump, briny morsel nestled between two shells just waiting for you to throw over the embers. Drink, pop, and eat!

Oysters Bonfire Baked with Bacon & Charred Onion

Serves 2

12 fresh oysters in the shell
6 strips good-quality thick-cut bacon
1 onion, sliced into rings
Splash of white wine for each oyster and yourself

There is something about smoked bacon and oysters that just works. It's one of the things that will never go out of style, like tartar sauce. Usually, baked oysters are done on the half shell in the oven or broiler. But I am assuming you are sitting by a bonfire on the beach, so we will do this a little differently.

Nestle the oysters around the hot coals of the fire. Using a handmade BBQ stick or a store-bought metal one, thread the slices of bacon onto the stick and roast over the flame just like a marshmallow until fully cooked but not crispy. Do the same with the onions, and cook until they take on a char and become caramelized.

Watch the oysters; if the liquor begins to bubble from the shell, pull immediately. You don't want the nectar to escape. Pull all the oysters from the coals, and carefully pry the oysters open from the lip side using an oyster knife and a towel; they will be hot. Pry open only far enough to expose the oyster; do not take off the shell. With the shell slightly open, break up some of the bacon and onion and place in the shell with a splash of the wine. Close the shell and set it back alongside the coals for just a couple more minutes.

When done, carefully remove the top shell and enjoy.

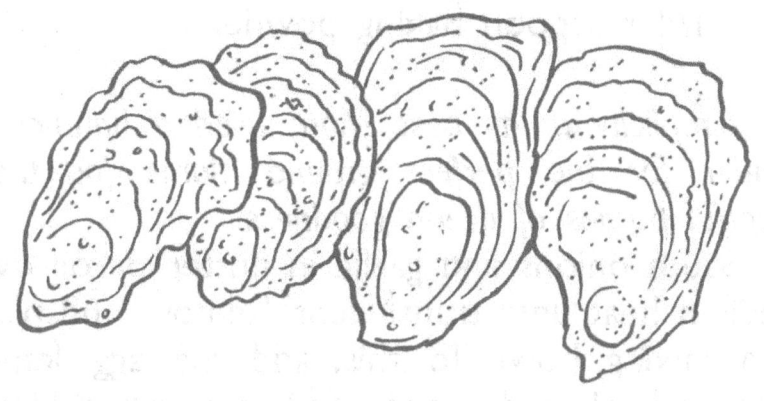

Northwest Clam Fritters

Serves 3

2 tablespoons minced onion
2 teaspoons minced garlic
Butter or oil, for sautéing
1 large egg
2 teaspoons lemon juice
Pinch of salt and white pepper
1-1/2 pounds finely chopped clam meat
1/4 cup ground soda crackers
1/4 teaspoon baking powder

Simplicity at its best. Mom used a hand-crank grinder for the perfect ground clams for these flavorful patties of ocean goodness.

Sauté onions and garlic in butter or oil over medium heat until translucent. Remove and place in a mixing bowl. To this, add the egg, lemon juice, and salt and pepper and mix well. Add the clams and stir well. Add the soda crackers and baking powder and combine thoroughly.

Dip your hands in water; then hand-scoop about 2 tablespoons of clam mixture and pat it into a 3/4-inch patty. Repeat until the batter is all used. Fry each side in butter over moderate heat until golden brown.

Serve with **My Favorite Tartar Sauce.**

Chilled Steamers with Lemon, Dill & Olive Oil

Serves 2

1/4 cup extra virgin olive oil

2 large cloves garlic, finely minced
1 tablespoon chili flakes
3 pounds steamer clams
Juice of 1/2 lemon
2 tablespoons fresh dill, finely chopped

Steamer clams are generally thought of as being served hot out of the sauté pan or steaming broth. I like to also serve them chilled for appetizers, neatly arranged on a platter.

In a sauté pan with a lid, add enough olive oil to lightly cover the bottom. Bring the oil to a moderate heat and add garlic and chili flakes. Give a quick sauté.

Now add steamers to the pan and cover with the lid. After a minute, check to see if the shells have popped. Pour cooked steamers and pan juice into a bowl. Add lemon juice and dill to steamers and stir well but carefully, so you don't separate the meat from the shells. Place in refrigerator until chilled; then serve.

Steamers Sautéed with Sake & Nori Butter

Serves 2

1/4 cup butter, softened
1 sheet nori
2 pounds steamer clams
1 cup sake
A squeeze of lime

What a great little snack in a shell—steamers or Manila clams found and raked locally on the Willapa Bay in Washington make for some amazing bonfire parties with local beer, garlic bread, and all the steamers you can eat. This recipe is a departure from the traditional "steaming" method, which tends to dilute the natural briny sea flavor of these little morsels. A side note: the indigenous clam was called a "littleneck," of which not many remain, but they are making a comeback thanks to a handful of oystermen in the Northwest. Manila clams hitched a ride over on the ships in the 1930s with the Japanese oysters transplanted on our shores. The Manila clams took a strong foothold and have flourished ever since, along with its Japanese oyster shipmate.

In a small blender, add the butter and sheet of nori and blend until butter becomes smooth and no pieces of nori remain.

In a sauté pan over moderate heat, add 2 tablespoons of the blended nori butter. Add steamers to the pan and sauté until their shells are coated well with butter. Now add the sake and squeeze of lime. Continue sautéing until all the shells have opened. Discard any shells that will not open.

Warm the remaining butter and use for dipping. Serve immediately.

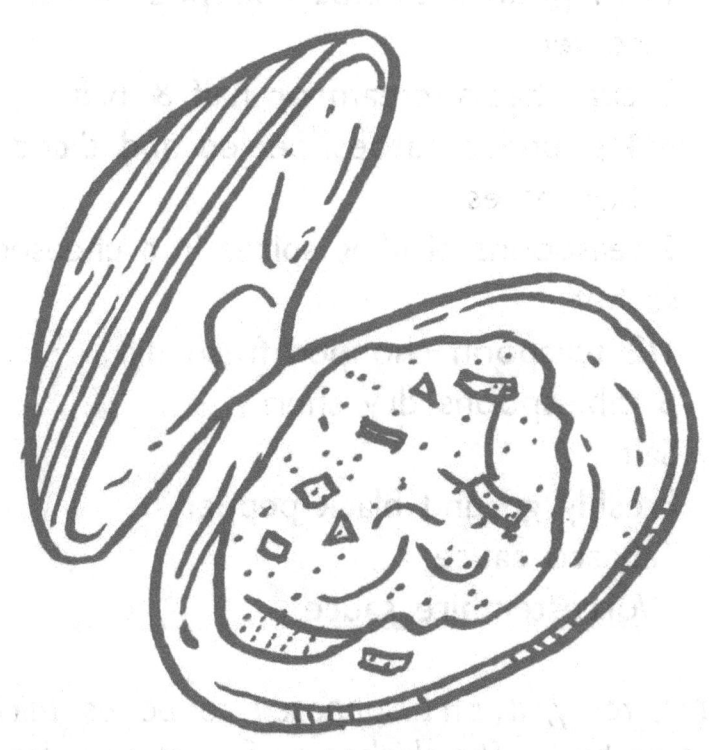

Clam Chowder

Serves 4

3 bacon slices, minced
1 tablespoon butter
1 small onion, diced
2 ribs celery, diced
2 tablespoons all-purpose flour
4 cups canned or bottled clam juice
1-1/4 pounds canned chopped clams, juice reserved
3 cups heavy cream or half & half
3/4 pound potatoes, peeled and diced
2 bay leaves
2 teaspoons pickling spices in a cheesecloth sachet
1/2 teaspoon chopped fresh dill
6 tablespoons dry sherry
Salt
Freshly ground black pepper
Tabasco sauce
Worcestershire sauce

No, really, it isn't supposed to be as thick as wallpaper paste. The thickness of most chowders has a tendency to mask the briny sea flavor of the clams and clam juice. For this recipe, we let the natural potato starch take the place of a thick roux.

Cook the bacon slowly in a soup pot over medium heat until lightly crisp, about 8 minutes. Do not drain bacon fat. Add the butter. Add the onion and celery to the bacon and grease and cook, stirring occasionally, until the onion is translucent, about 5 to 7 minutes. Add the flour and cook over low heat, stirring with a wooden spoon, for 2 to 3 minutes.

Whisk in 4 cups of clam juice until smooth. Add clams and reserved juice, bring to a simmer, and cook for 5 minutes, stirring occasionally. Add the cream, potatoes, bay leaves, pickling spice sachet, and fresh dill. Simmer on low until potatoes are tender.

Stir in the sherry. Add salt, pepper, Tabasco, and Worcestershire sauce, all to taste.

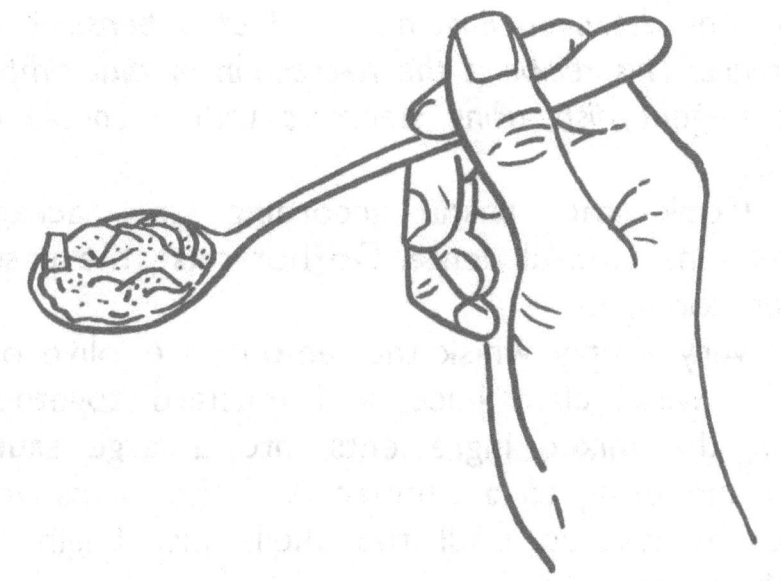

Clam Linguine My Way

Serves 2

About 6 ounces dry linguine
Juice of 1/4 lemon
4 tablespoons extra virgin olive oil
2 large cloves garlic, minced
4 tablespoons dry white wine (no oak, please)
1 cup clam juice
1 tablespoon Dijon mustard
2 pounds steamer clams
1/3 cup chopped fresh Italian parsley

One of my fondest memories from a trip to Italy was the clam linguine I had at a pensione in Florence. This recipe is the re-creation of that simple but elegant dish, using steamers with a couple of twists.

Cook the pasta according to package directions until al dente. Do not rinse the pasta after cooking.

Very simply whisk the lemon juice, olive oil, garlic, wine, clam juice, and mustard together. Pour the mixed ingredients into a large sauté pan and bring to a simmer. Add the clams and cook uncovered until the shells just begin to slightly open.

Add the linguine and toss with parsley. Once all the steamers have opened, serve.

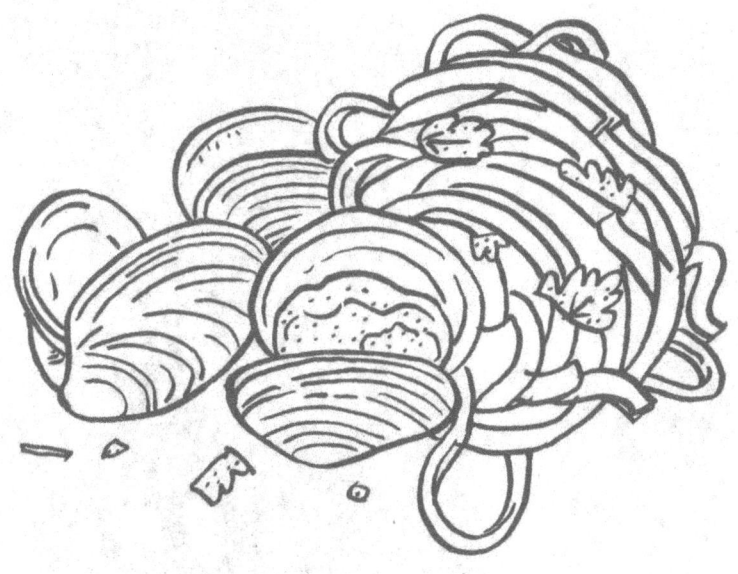

Photo from Shutterstock

A Fish Story

The giant prehistoric sturgeon feeding on the sandy bottom of the lower Columbia River was not safe when Gus dropped the anchor of his little bowpicker. You see, Gus, not unlike Dr. Doolittle, seemed to be able to talk to the sturgeon and know just where and what they were dining on for breakfast, lunch, and dinner. His talent for dropping just the right bait in front of the nose of a hungry sturgeon gave him quite the reputation as a guide to hook and land the gray-and-white armor-plated swimming dinosaurs.

As Gus's popularity grew, the number of guided trips to the sturgeon grounds increased. Gus needed a deckhand, and I knew just the right person—me! At fourteen, I was always looking for an odd job to buy fireworks and gas for the motorcycle. Deckhanding for Gus seemed like a regular odd job to make a quick buck, but of course, it wasn't very regular.

To begin, in the days of James Dean and fast motorcycles, Gus would ride his black-and-chrome Indian with cool and rebellious abandon. He would take on all white-T-shirt-with-cigarettes-rolled-in-the-sleeve challengers to race on the hard-packed sand of the world's longest driving beach. After a string of merciless wins, Gus had one last, unfortunate race. An overcast day dominated the sky as the outgoing tide revealed the hard-packed sand drag strip where Gus had raced to victory many times. The sound of the waves crashing against the sandbar was completely overshadowed by the rumble of the two Indian motorcycles roaring down the beach as fast as they could go, with Gus in the lead like usual. Eying the finish line, Gus could hear the challenger advancing and gave the throttle one last desperate twist to propel him and the Indian to a safe margin of victory. That's when it happened: the front wheel of the speeding bike hit a small ripple in the unforgiving sand, and Gus violently laid the raging Indian over and tumbled just short of the finish as the other bike sped to victory. Gus lay crumpled and intertwined with his bike, both legs severely fractured. He was rushed to the hospital, where, at the time, the only solution was to amputate both legs.

As the handful of passengers for the day's fishing trip gathered at the top of the ramp leading down to the dock, I helped push Gus in his wheelchair from his nearby house to the waiting one-day fishermen. The best time to go sturgeon fishing is at low tide, and the low water made the slope of the ramp leading down to the boat slips look like an amusement ride. With the eager fishermen at the top of the steep forty-foot ramp looking on, I positioned myself and Gus at the top, holding on for dear life to the two handles on the back of his chair. Pointing Gus straight down the middle of the slippery wooden pathway, I slowly pushed the wheelchair over the precipice, knowing I only had one shot at reaching the bottom or we'd fall into the drink. Using my feet as brakes while holding on to the chair and Gus, we slid slowly at first and then got faster and faster until we thudded a hard hit at the bottom, where the steep ramp intersected the flat dock way leading to the boat. Once we were at the bottom, the rest of the passengers carefully made their way down the ramp, and we all trundled to the little bowpicker waiting to take us fishing.

The bowpicker, named *Neap Tide*, was originally designed to lay out long gill nets to catch the mighty salmon of the Columbia River but now enjoyed retirement fishing for sturgeon where it once pulled in nets filled with silver gold. A small makeshift ramp lay beside *Neap Tide*; I picked this up and laid it down on the gunwales of the boat to create a ramp to wheel Gus up to the helm from the dock. Once he was settled in at the helm, I helped the rest of the passengers in and cast off the lines. With a stubborn chug from the little diesel engine, the drab wooden-hulled *Neap Tide* made its way out of the harbor past the awesome-looking fiberglass charter boats with brightly colored hull paint and names like *Salmon Slayer* or *Wave Runner*. Too bad those paying customers on the fancy boats wouldn't catch nearly as many sturgeon as we would.

Making the run to the fishing grounds, I geared up the poles for each person with the guidance of Gus's uncanny ability to read the conditions of the water and weather and what the sturgeon wanted for breakfast that day. A wave of nostalgia came over all in the boat passing the skeleton-looking pilings, the remains of the big salmon canneries perched above the Columbia where *Neap Tide* once delivered its salmon catches.

"Okay, ready, Gus," I said, as all the poles were ready to go. "Let's drop anchor." As Gus positioned the little boat, I made ready the anchor and waited for his command to drop it by hand—no fancy winches here.

"Okay, drop it, kid!" Down it splashed through the green waters to about forty feet.

"Back her down, Gus, and set the hook," I said. Then it was done. I was now ready to get the lines wet. I went to each eager person, handed them a pole, and gave them a quick lesson on how to set the hook when a sturgeon bit and how not to get a rat's nest of line on the reel when lowering the bait to the bottom.

"Hey, Gus, is it fresh anchovy or smelt today?"

"No, no," he said, "I think we need my special bait." And of course, he was right. Gus's special bait was sitting in the bilge, the intestines of the boat, soaking up all the good smells the little *Neap Tide* had to offer.

I always loved the look of anticipation on the passengers' faces for a huge sturgeon to bite their hook, trusting us to know what the sturgeon wanted. I pulled out the stinky, smelly special bait. It generally worked, and not long after running the leader through the body of the stinky smelt with the hook out the mouth and dropping it to the bottom, we had our first fish. First a little nibble, then a little bigger one ... wait ... wait ... I coached the excited customer. I was waiting for just the right strength of pull from the sturgeon below.

"Now! Set the hook!" With a steady, hard jerk, the hook was set. "Keep the tip of your pole up," I said.

"Don't give him any slack."

"Gus, where's the net?"

"In the stern, boy." By the time I retrieved the net, the sturgeon had been reeled close to the boat and the fisherman's anticipation was palpable.

"Ease it here, slowly, don't horse him, take it easy. There it is. Pull the tip, pull up, that's it." As I slipped the net under the five-footer, cheers erupted from the boat and a smile came across Gus's face. I think the little *Neap Tide,* at that moment, also felt joy in its retirement.

That day we caught four of the large prehistoric fish, and all passengers satisfied, it was time to pull anchor and head home. I couldn't help thinking that maybe retirement wasn't so bad for the little bowpicker, run by a legless man who seemed to be able to talk to sturgeon and loved the little boat.

Buying Sturgeon

The first thing you will want to ask your fishmonger is a little different than other fish. You will stroll up to the counter and ask how fresh the sturgeon is. And if he or she says it was caught yesterday ... well, wait. You see, sturgeon is one of the few fish you do want a bit of age on. I always let my sturgeon hang in a cool place for a minimum of three days. The flesh of the sturgeon is very, very firm and still quite "alive" for quite some time after landing it on the boat. As a matter of fact, when filleting a sturgeon, it is common for the meat to jump and curl while cutting it. The meat needs to rest for a while to become tender. If you cook sturgeon when it is too fresh, it will scrunch up and seize, creating a tough piece of fish for the dinner plate.

Today sturgeon, for the most part, is farmed. When selecting a piece of sturgeon, it should be mainly white, without any graying or dark browning. Farmed sturgeon tends to have a strong-tasting layer of yellowish fat. I recommend removing as much of this as you can because the flavor can be quite muddy.

Sturgeon and Dumplings

Serves 2 to 4

- 2 pounds white sturgeon
- 2 ribs celery, diced
- 1 small yellow onion, sliced
- 4 cloves garlic, minced
- 2 small carrots, diced
- 4 bay leaves
- 12 whole cloves
- 2 tablespoons butter
- 2 cups dry white wine
- 2 quarts clam juice or chicken stock
- Salt and pepper
- Dumpling dough (see recipe below)

Dumplings:

- 2 cups all-purpose flour
- 4 teaspoons baking powder
- Pinch of salt
- 2 tablespoons butter, softened
- 3/4 cup milk

Because of the sturgeon's dense texture, it is the perfect "chicken of the sea" for this dumpling dish.

Cut the sturgeon into thick 2-inch chunks and set aside.

Using a shallow pot with a heavy bottom, sauté the celery, onion, garlic, carrots, bay leaves, and cloves in butter until the onion becomes translucent. Add the wine and clam juice and bring to a low simmer. Add salt and pepper to taste.

For the dumplings, sift the flour, baking powder, and salt into a large mixing bowl. Using a dough cutter or fork, cut the butter into the dry ingredients until well blended but lumpy. Add the milk and mix until you have a sticky dough.

Add the chunks of sturgeon to the simmering liquid. Dust your hands with flour, pull golf ball–size portions of dough from the bowl, and drop into the simmering stew. *Do not roll or form your dumplings; just pull and drop.* When all the dumpling mixture has been used, cover the pot and simmer for 15 to 20 minutes, or until dumplings become firm and not mushy.

Serve hot in deep bowls.

Oven-Braised Sturgeon with Salt Pork

Serves 4

1/2 pound salt pork or thick slab bacon, cut into 1-inch pieces
1 small yellow onion, cut into large chunks
1 carrot, diced large
2 ribs celery, diced large
1 tablespoon whole black peppercorns
2 anchovy fillets, finely minced
2 pounds white sturgeon, cut to fit in skillet
All-purpose flour, for dredging
1/2 cup Aquavit
2 cups clam juice
Juice of 1/2 lemon
1/2 teaspoon brown sugar
1 tablespoon pickling spice, wrapped loosely and tied in cheesecloth

A cast iron skillet works great for this recipe to create a one-pot meal.

In a deep cast iron skillet, sauté the slab pork until all sides are brown. Add the onion, carrot, celery, peppercorns, and anchovies and continue sautéing until onion becomes translucent. Push the sautéed ingredients to one side of the pan.

Dredge the sturgeon in flour. On the clear side of the skillet, using the bacon grease remaining, brown each side of the sturgeon and cover with sautéed ingredients. Pour Aquavit into the skillet. Once it comes to a simmer, add clam juice, lemon juice, brown sugar, and pickling spice bundle. Cover and braise in the oven at 350°F for up to 1 hour.

Serve with boiled potatoes or hardtack crackers.

Crawdads Boiled in Dill

Serves a few or a crowd

The following measurements are for each quart of water:
1/4 cup or a touch less of rock salt or other good-quality salt
1 large crowned sprig of dill
1 tablespoon brown sugar
1/2 bottle dark beer (least amount of hops)
2 tablespoons lemon juice
1/2 tablespoon pickling spices
Crawdads

Crawdads from the lower Columbia River are some of the biggest and best tasting around. In fact, some of them are so big that the claws pose a threat to your fingers if you're not careful. Grandpa, of course, being from Sweden was the master of crawdad population control. But he also had the uncanny knack for taking the most unruly and mean crawdad out of the bucket and putting it to sleep by rubbing its belly, a mystic technique that still eludes me.

Estimate how many quarts of water you will need to completely cover the crawdads you want to cook.

Add all ingredients except crawdads to a pot and bring to a boil. Add the crawdads and bring water back to a rolling boil and cook for 3 to 5 minutes; then turn off the heat and let the crawdads soak for another 10 minutes. Drain and serve.

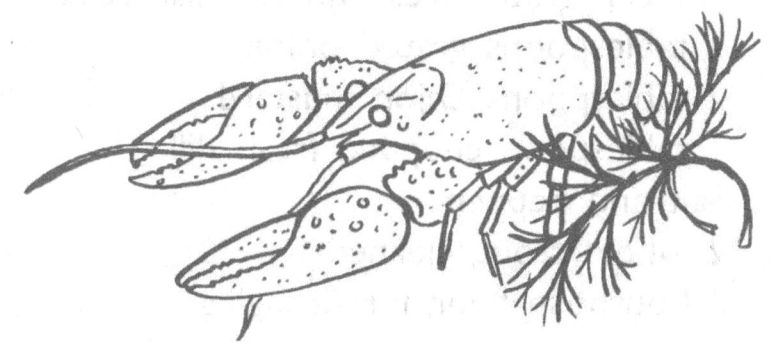

Horseradish Trout

Serves 2

1/4 cup grated fresh horseradish root
2 tablespoons grated onion
2 tablespoons Dijon mustard
1 tablespoon chopped fresh dill
Salt and pepper
2 whole trout, cleaned
All-purpose flour, for dredging

For adding an extra little kick to your fresh-caught trout, you must try this on your next catch. Use only fresh horseradish with this recipe. You'll find it at most supermarkets.

Mix the horseradish, onion, mustard, dill, and salt and pepper to taste.

Dredge the trout in flour and slather horseradish mixture on each side.

Bake in a 375°F oven for approximately 15 to 20 minutes, flipping the trout halfway through cooking.

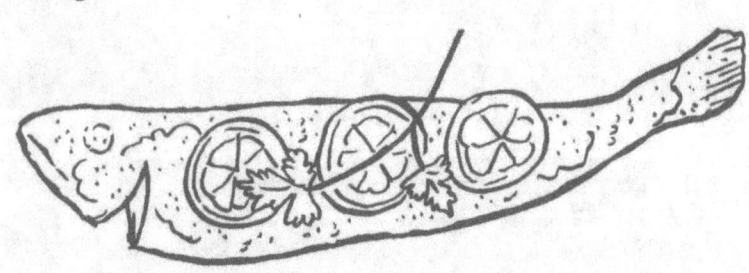

Stuffed and Fried Squid With Scallops and Shrimp

Serves 4

1/2 cup scallops
1 egg white
2 teaspoons cornstarch
1 teaspoon lemon juice
1/2 teaspoon vodka
1 small clove garlic, finely minced
Pinch of salt
Pinch of white pepper
1/4 cup peeled, deveined, and tail removed Pacific pink shrimp
1 teaspoon finely chopped chives
12 squid tubes
Pinch of smoked sea salt

The tube-like body of the squid was made to fill. Be creative and have fun with this at your next barbecue.

In a food processor, blend the scallops, egg white, and cornstarch until smooth. Add the lemon juice, vodka, garlic, salt, and pepper, and blend until incorporated. Remove scallop mixture and transfer to a bowl. Gently stir in shrimp meat and chives.

Fit a pastry bag with a round tip to fit the opening of the squid. Fill the pastry bag with the scallop mixture. One at a time, pipe the mixture into the squid tubes. Do not completely fill the tubes, because the scallop mixture will expand when cooking and rip the tubes if overfilled. Close the open ends of the squid tubes with a toothpick. Coat the filled tubes with olive oil and a sprinkle of smoked sea salt.

Grill lightly, until the filling feels firm. Let grilled squid stand for a couple of minutes; then slice into rounds for presentation.

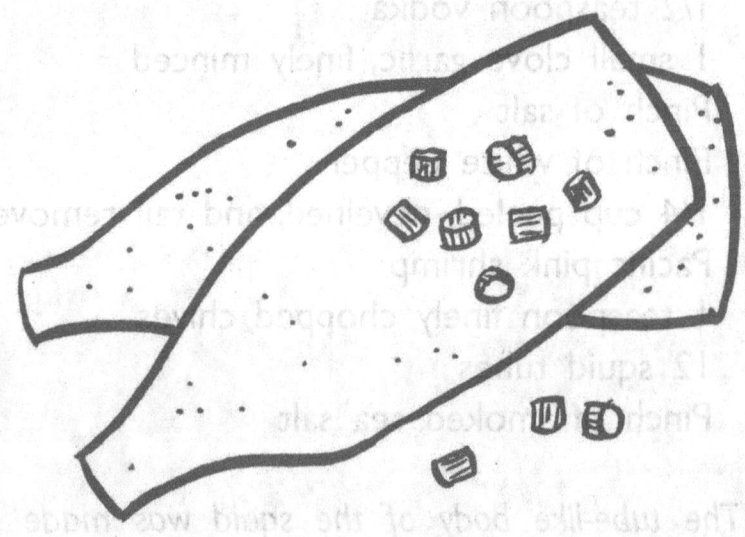

Salt and Pepper Smelt

Serves 4

10 smelt, innards removed (or not)
1 cup soy sauce
1 cup cornstarch
2 cups rice flour
2 tablespoons Kosher salt
2 tablespoons coarse black pepper
Frying oil
2 to 3 dried hot chiles, chopped

Using very long dip nets to catch the wiggling silver masses of smelt heading upstream was great fun. There were so many ways to use these little rich-tasting gems, from smoking to pickling, frying, and of course, they made the best sturgeon bait.

This recipe is reminiscent of the classic salt and pepper shrimp found at many Asian restaurants.

Begin by soaking the smelt in soy sauce for at least 30 minutes.

In a bowl, make a dry mix of the cornstarch, rice flour, salt, and pepper.

In a sauté pan, heat the oil with chiles until fragrant. Remove smelt from soy sauce and dredge thoroughly in the dry mixture. Fry the smelt in hot oil with chiles still in it until golden brown on each side.

Photo from Shutterstock

A Story on Land

A John Deere tractor, affectionately referred to as a "Johnny Popper," was my tractor in training. I was always told the nickname referred to the noise of the exhaust, but I was sure the name had came from the ability of the open flywheel and belt to pop off a finger, or something worse. Down the road from my house lived a grizzly old farmer who had a lifelong obsession with the bottle, which had taken its toll. Unable to tend to the hay farm that sprawled below his double-wide trailer, he had to hire a farmhand, who was generally me.

The first season I chose to defect from the slick stainless and tile farm down the road was the season I met my match: the Johnny Popper. "Can you run one of these?" he asked, pointing with a shaky finger.

"Uh, sure, no

problem," too embarrassed and stubborn to say, "What the hell is that?"

"Good. Then, ted the hay."

As I hopped on and cranked her over with all the confidence of a plumber performing brain surgery, I realized I hadn't a clue how to coax this beast into doing my bidding. "Hey, it has been awhile; could you give me a refresher?" Been awhile ... I had to laugh at that. What's a while when I hadn't even hit puberty and still thought the neighbor farm girl was icky. But with a quick refresher course from a very inebriated teacher, I was off, weaving down the muddy path to the hayfields sprawling before me, thinking to myself, *This is going to be a really long day.*

I was a very quick learner, though, and my windrows were quite admirable. I must say, I think that old green tractor and I became good friends. It allowed me to keep all of my legs, arms, toes, and fingers and I, in return, treated it with kindness and respect. Heck, if I didn't think the farm girl next door would have given me cooties, I may have even taken her for a ride.

Dairy farms dotted the inland adjacent to the Columbia River, and when I wasn't fishing, crabbing, or clam digging, I was working on the hayfields. By the age of ten, I began bucking the bales of grass hay that would soon be food for the milk-producing Holsteins of the farm. Bucking bales was nothing to be taken lightly; if you were at all worth your weight in farm boy salt, you threw yourself into this rite of passage as soon as possible. The bucking crew was always made up of a couple of big, strapping farm boys with serious attitudes, sporting premature body hair and sinewy muscles. With a spat of tobacco and a guttural grunt, these boys could buck and clear the four-foot-high flatbed and land the bale atop a stack eight high. Wow, I thought; now that must be when you get to be a man and show the neighbor girl the hay fort you just built!

As I walked alongside the moving flatbed truck positioning for the next row of bales, I knew what I had to do: since I was half the age of the tobacco-spitting, eight-high bucking man boys, maybe if I could buck a bale four high, they might tell me the secret of sprouting chin hair and growing taut muscles, not to mention letting me have a dip. I ran ahead of the half-loaded flatbed, positioning myself on the next bale, grabbing both twines with both hands, waiting for the right moment. The truck moved slowly, waiting for me to buck that hay five high. I jerked the bale, knowing the man-boys were watching, and bounced it off my knee to get enough momentum to push the bale over my head. With outstretched arms as far and as hard as they could push towards the sky, I could taste the chew, I could feel my muscles tighten; I could picture my hay fort with the farm girl next door drinking lemonade in it! Yes! SNAP! No! With a sound like a balloon popping, the two twines let go of their sturdy grip on the compact grass hay just as the bale reached the top of my head. Momentarily blinded by the dusty fallout, I tripped over the bale next to me and landed face up with the remainder of the hay falling from the sky and covering my ten-year-old frame.

Lying there humiliated and hoping the hay had somehow made me disappear, I felt a leather strap of a hand yank me up by the belt. "Nice try, kid," said one of the man-boys, "but why don't you just drive the truck?"

"Sure," I said weakly. I got up, brushed myself off and jumped in the cab. "Uh, does anyone have a bucket to sit on?" I asked. I can barely see over the wheel." "Sure, hang on," said the man-boy. "Here. You wanna dip while I get it?" "You bet," I said. *Wow, all right,* I thought to myself, as I put a little dip in my cheek. *Man, that it is good.* When the man-boy returned with the bucket, I was really glad and a bit anxious to get it out of his hands—well, not with excitement to sit on it and drive, but to throw up in it from the foul tobacco in my mouth. Maybe the lemonade and hay fort were still a possibility, I thought. I bet I only need to buck the bale two high for that.

Mom's Swedish Meatballs

Serves 4

1/2 cup roughly chopped onion
2 cups cubed day-old white bread
1/4 cup half & half
2 eggs
1/4 teaspoon ground allspice
Pinch of salt
1/2 teaspoon black pepper
3/4 pound unseasoned ground pork
3/4 pound ground beef
2 tablespoons butter for frying the meatballs

For Sauce:

2 tablespoons all-purpose flour
2 cups beef broth
Dash of Worcestershire
Pinch of white pepper
1/2 teaspoon granulated onion
1/4 teaspoon ground allspice
Pinch of salt
1/4 cup heavy cream

Svenska kottbuller, *or Swedish meatballs, were a staple growing up. They were served with lingonberry preserves, marinated cucumbers, and little new potatoes. Yes, size does matter when rolling these world-renowned little balls of beef pork. Not quite as large as their Italian counterpart, they are more like the size of a small Super Ball or just a touch bigger than a quarter.*

In a food processor or blender, add the onion and blend until smooth or liquefied. To this, add the bread, half & half, eggs, allspice, salt, and pepper; blend thoroughly.

In a bowl, combine the pork and beef with the bread mixture, using your hands, until all ingredients are incorporated and smooth. With wet hands, roll meatballs into very small balls about 1 1/2 inches across.

In a heavy-bottomed skillet on medium heat, melt the butter and fry the meatballs until golden brown and cooked all the way through. Remove meatballs and set aside. Reserve the skillet without cleaning it for making the sauce.

In the same skillet you used for the meatballs, with the butter and brown bits still in it, add the flour and whisk until totally incorporated. Pour in the beef broth and whisk well. Add the Worcestershire, white pepper, granulated onion, allspice, and salt, and whisk well. Pour in cream and very lightly simmer until the sauce is thick.

Place meatballs in sauce and serve.

Fish Dumpling Soup

Serves 4 to 5

For the fish dumplings:

1 pound cod, cut into large cubes and blended in a food processor
1 egg white
2 tablespoons heavy cream
2 tablespoons cornstarch
1 tablespoon minced green onion
2 teaspoons finely minced garlic
1 teaspoon soy sauce
White pepper to taste

For the soup:

Vegetable oil, for sautéing
1 small onion, diced
1 tablespoon minced ginger
4 large cloves garlic, minced
1 to 2 dried hot chile peppers
2 quarts clam juice
1 can coconut milk
3 tablespoons fish sauce
1/2 cup dry sherry

3 tablespoons rice vinegar
2 tablespoons soy sauce
3 tablespoons sweet chili sauce
Chopped fresh cilantro, for garnish

Not only is this soup a unique crowd pleaser, but it's also very healthy—a must-try in place of the everyday chicken soup on a cold day. Add as much pepper heat as you want; it's up to you.

Blend cod, egg white, and cream until smooth. Add all other dumpling ingredients and blend until well incorporated.

Heat a little oil in a heavy-bottomed soup pot over medium heat; sweat the onion, ginger, and garlic. Break up the chile peppers and add to the pot; sauté until they become aromatic. Add the clam juice and then all remaining ingredients, except the cilantro. Let simmer for 15 to 20 minutes then strain, reserving the liquid to make the dumpling soup.

Bring the reserved soup to a low simmer.

Using a teaspoon dipped in water, scoop out a small amount of the fish dumpling mixture and carefully drop into the simmering soup. (The dumplings don't have to be a perfect ball shape; as a matter of fact, a bit rougher shape tends to better pick up the flavor of the soup and has a more interesting texture). Drop in as many as you want and simmer fish dumplings until they are firm, a minimum of 10 minutes. A longer simmer is great because the dumplings will absorb the flavor of the soup.

Garnish with cilantro and serve.

Chilled Fiddlehead Fern Salad

Serves 4

Salted boiling water
1 tablespoon pickling spice, wrapped and tied in cheesecloth
2 cups fresh-picked fiddlehead ferns, any dried, outer shell-like material removed
2 tablespoons white vinegar
1 tablespoon sugar
Pinch of salt
1/2 teaspoon white pepper
Bowl of ice water
4 large red radishes, sliced paper thin
1/4 small red onion, very thinly sliced
1/2 cup watercress leaves
1/2 tablespoon finely chopped fresh dill

If you are looking for something that tastes like walking through the deep, dense, wet, sun-blocked green forests of the Pacific Coast Range, this is it. You can find fiddleheads in the spring at specialty markets or farmers markets.

In salted boiling water with the pickling spice, poach fiddlehead ferns for 7 minutes, or until just barely tender.

While fiddleheads are poaching, make a dressing by combining the vinegar, sugar, salt, and white pepper in a small bowl; stir until sugar has dissolved. Set aside.

When fiddleheads are just tender, remove from the cooking water and plunge into ice water; chill completely. Toss the chilled fiddleheads with the radishes, onion, watercress, and dill. Dress with vinegar dressing and toss.

Marinated Cucumbers

Serves 4

1/2 to 3/4 cup white vinegar
3 to 4 tablespoons sugar
1/4 teaspoon salt
2 tablespoons water
2 tablespoons finely chopped baby dill
2 cucumbers, peeled and thinly sliced

A staple of my childhood and a constant in my refrigerator, the clean, crisp flavor of marinated cucumbers goes with just about everything in my book. I think I will quit writing for a bite of leftover fish cakes from last night and marinated cucumbers on hardtack, with a touch of mustard.

In a nonreactive bowl, combine all ingredients except cucumbers and stir until the sugar is dissolved. Add the cucumbers and let stand for a minimum of 1 hour. Cucumbers are at their best when marinated overnight.

Lingonberry & Sweet Onion Compote

Makes about 1-1/2 cups

4 tablespoons butter, divided
1 medium Walla Walla sweet onion, halved and thinly sliced
4 to 6 whole cloves
2 large bay leaves
1 cup lingonberry preserves
1 tablespoon brown sugar
2 tablespoons Aquavit
1/4 cup cranberry juice
1/4 cup red wine vinegar
Salt and pepper

You can find lingonberry preserves at most specialty food stores.

In a skillet over medium heat, melt 3 tablespoons butter and sauté the onion with cloves and bay leaves until the onions become slightly caramelized. Add the lingonberries and brown sugar; stir well. Reduce heat to low and pour in the Aquavit, cranberry juice, and vinegar. Let simmer for 5 to 7 minutes, or until the compote becomes thick. Finish compote with 1 tablespoon butter. Add salt and pepper to taste.

Nori Spaetzle

Serves 4

1 cup all-purpose flour
1/2 sheet toasted nori, very finely chopped
Pinch of white pepper
1/2 teaspoon salt
1/4 cup milk
2 eggs
1/4 teaspoon sesame oil
1 gallon salted water, boiling

You will need a spaetzle maker, which can be found at most kitchen stores, for this recipe.

In one bowl, mix the flour, nori, pepper, and salt.

In another bowl mix the milk, eggs, and sesame oil. Pour the milk mixture into the flour mixture, combining well until dough is wet and smooth.

With the spaetzle maker sitting over the boiling water, load the spaetzle dough into the hopper and slide back and forth slowly to drop the little dumplings into the boiling water. When the spaetzle float back to the top, let cook for another 30 seconds then remove with a slotted spoon. Spread spaetzle on a sheet pan to cool.

Sauté in butter and serve alongside your favorite seafood dish.

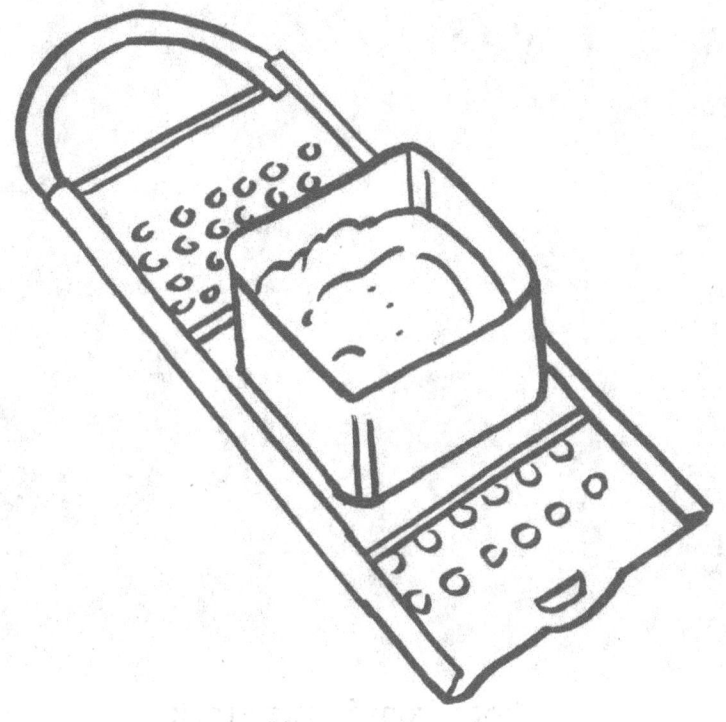

Photo from Shutterstock

My Favorite Tartar Sauce

Makes about 1-1/2 cups

2 cups good-quality mayonnaise
1/2 cup sour cream
1/4 cup buttermilk
1 tablespoon chopped dill
2 teaspoons finely minced anchovy
1 teaspoon finely minced capers
1 teaspoon caper brine
1 tablespoon finely minced green onion tops and bottoms
1 teaspoon finely minced garlic (mash with a touch of salt with side of knife into paste)
Juice of 1/2 lemon
1/2 teaspoon Tabasco sauce
1/4 teaspoon celery salt
1 hard-boiled egg, finely chopped

There are just some things on this earth that make it more enjoyable to be part of this planet—family, love, fishing, clam digging, peace, and a good tartar sauce. Not necessarily in that order. I love my family, but mom doesn't forget to make the tartar sauce when I come to visit.

In a mixing bowl, add mayonnaise, sour cream, and buttermilk; whisk until smooth. Add remaining ingredients, except the egg, and blend well. Once all ingredients are blended, gently fold in the egg.

Huckleberry Mustard

Makes a generous quart

2 cups brown mustard seeds
1/4 cup water
2-3/4 cups white vinegar
1 cup huckleberries
1/2 cup brown sugar
1/2 teaspoon ground allspice
1/4 teaspoon ground ginger
1/2 teaspoon ground cardamom
Pinch of salt

If huckleberries are not available, use blueberries. Once you have the basic recipe down, start adding whatever your food imagination can conjure.

In a nonreactive container, combine mustard seeds, water, and vinegar. Allow to sit overnight in the refrigerator to soften the seeds.

In a food processor or blender, blend mustard seeds with their soaking liquid until almost smooth but with some of the seeds left whole. Add all other ingredients and blend well, still leaving some of the mustard seeds whole.

Note: You can add more vinegar and brown sugar to achieve the texture you desire.

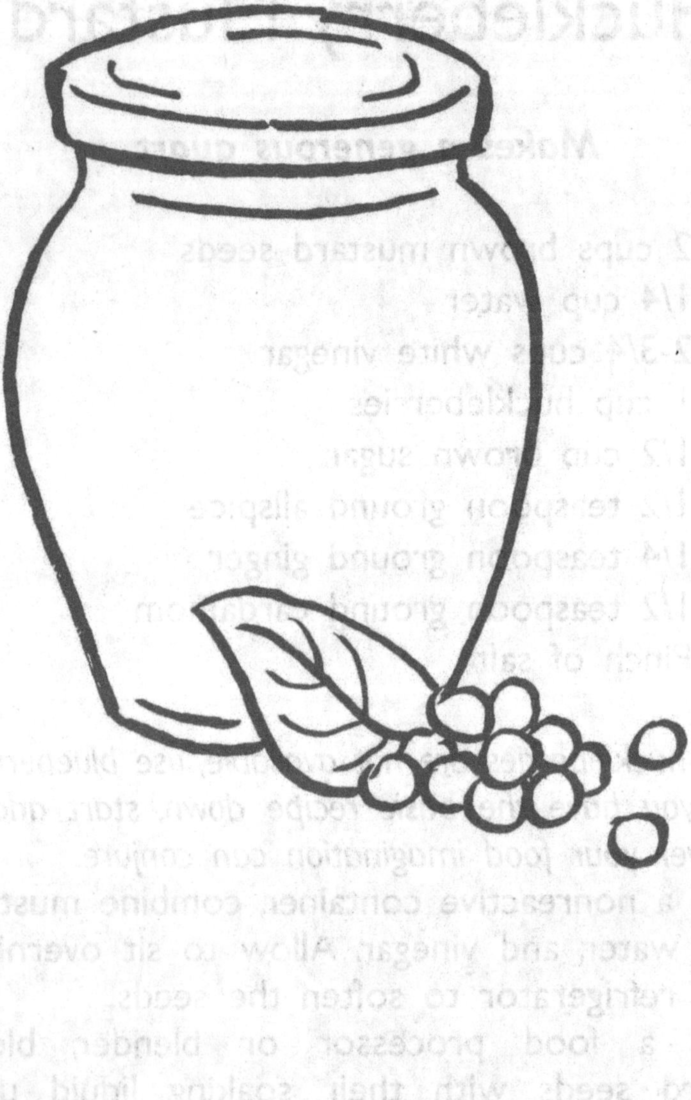

Horseradish AppleSauce

Makes about 2-1/2 cups

2 cups unsweetened applesauce
3 tablespoons sour cream
2 tablespoons prepared horseradish, more or less
2 teaspoons red wine vinegar
1 tablespoon brown sugar
1/2 teaspoon ground cardamom
Pinch of salt

A very simple recipe that is great on just about everything. I love the sweet heat and tanginess on the tongue.

Whisk all the ingredients together until the brown sugar is dissolved and incorporated.

Serve with your favorite pork dish, sausage, beef, or even a dense fish like a tuna steak.

Smoked Sea Salt

Makes 2 cups

2 cups course sea salt or large salt flakes
Enough cheesecloth to create a loose pouch for your salt (if cheesecloth is not available, you may use some sort of a fine-meshed colander)
String to tie
Completely dry wood chips, not soaked in water

If you have a smoker and want to add a new twist to your salt, try this easy-to-do recipe. I promise, you will be thinking of many ways to use your smoked salt. It is amazing how many different flavors you can achieve, between the types of salt available, the types of smoking materials you can use, and the length of the smoke.

Very simply wrap your salt in the cheesecloth extremely loosely so the smoke can circulate throughout the salt. Tie the pouch closed. The pouch should be loose enough to lie flat on your smoking rack.

Load your smoker with the wood chips and smoke on high, creating a full, heavy smoke. Place your salt on the rack of the smoker and continue a full, heavy smoke for at least 4 hours. Adjust the length of the smoke to achieve your desired flavor.

Glogg

Makes about 2-1/2 quarts

4 bottles sweet red wine (such as Port)
1/4 bottle whiskey
1/4 bottle vodka
6 whole cardamom pods, cracked
Peel of 1/2 orange, pith removed
2 cinnamon sticks
6 to 8 whole cloves
1/2 cup sugar
1/2 cup dried currants
1/2 cup blanched almonds

Ah, yes, Glogg. It may be fitting for it to be at the end of the recipes. There is nothing better than the complex warm spice and alcohol that tickles your tongue, warms your belly, and lightens your soul. A perfect end to a cool, rainy day of fishing or hunting on the North Oregon coast.

Combine all ingredients in a heavy-bottomed stockpot, reserving half of the orange peel, and slowly bring to a simmer. Simmer for 10 minutes. Meanwhile, slice the reserved orange peel and set aside.

Strain the liquid and serve in clear mugs garnished with the orange strips.

Acknowledgments

I extend my gratitude to those who nurtured me in the true Pacific Northwest way of life:

My mom, the chef who created the recipe that made me a student and devotee of all that is Pacific Northwest. This book is dedicated to her for teaching me how to dig razors and for cleaning and cooking them. For standing in the high weeds handing me shells out of her cooking apron so I could shoot the ducks in the sloughs below our house. She is a true Pacific Northwest mother, and I can only hope to pass on her love and passion to my children.

My stepfather, a true teacher of the Pacific Northwest way of life. He embodies the true Pacific Northwest experience, rich in colorful lore and authentic in character. A commercial fisherman, maritime instructor, and fisher poet, he is an amazing inspiration to me.

My wife, Jennifer, the love of my life, who always put up with my finding a way to get out of responsibility so I could hit the next clam tide or fishing hole. I thank her for her patience with me eating the "nasty" parts of the fish or hoofed animal; I know she longs for a "normal" meal. Above all, I thank her for supporting me as I teach our children all that is Pacific Northwest.

My three children, who are all great clam diggers and who I am way more than proud of. I hope they will carry on the traditions and culture while teaching their children all that is Pacific Northwest.

I thank my publicist, Sharon Cook, for her endless encouragement and confidence in me.

About the Author

John Nelson is an avid outdoorsman, chef, author, and food and beverage professional. He lives with his wife and three children in Eugene, Oregon, which is central to the mountains, ocean, and high desert. John is currently the chef at a Corvalis country club and works with a 125-year-old seafood company.

Volume Measurements		Weight Measurements		Temperature Conversion	
U.S.	Metric	U.S.	Metric	Fahrenheit	Celsius
1 teaspoon	5 ml	1/2 ounce	15 g	250	120
1 tablespoon	15 ml	1 ounce	30 g	300	150
1/4 cup	60 ml	3 ounces	90 g	325	160
1/3 cup	75 ml	4 ounces	115 g	350	180
1/2 cup	125 ml	8 ounces	225 g	375	190
2/3 cup	150 ml	12 ounces	350 g	400	200
3/4 cup	175 ml	1 pound	450 g	425	220
1 cup	250 ml	2-1/4 pounds	1 kg	450	230

www.ingramcontent.com/pod-product-compliance
Lightning Source LLC
Chambersburg PA
CBHW011306150426
43191CB00016B/2346